GLIMPSES OF EDEN

Field notes from the edge of eternity
A round-the-year anthology based on *The Tablet* column

JONATHAN TULLOCH

DARTON · LONGMAN + TODD

As ever for Shirley and Aidan

First published in 2018 by
Darton, Longman and Todd Ltd
1 Spencer Court
140 – 142 Wandsworth High Street
London SW18 4JJ

Reprinted 2018

ISBN:978-0-232-53380-4

Designed and produced by Judy Linard
Printed and bound in Great Britain by Bell & Bain, Glasgow

Contents

Foreword

For nearly twenty years, we have been living in the heart of North Yorkshire's Herriot country with its little hills, hidden valleys and secretive woods. Every week, I write a nature column called 'Glimpses of Eden' for *The Tablet* magazine.

This book is a selection from nearly a thousand of my *Tablet* columns. I have arranged them into seasons to capture the rhythm of the year, with eight per month. Accompanying each piece is my recent response when revisiting the columns, in some cases written many years ago. This process has been personally surprising, moving and uplifting.

Unable to drive and rarely travelling far, most of this book is what I have encountered within an hour's bike ride of home.

Winter

Lurking in the twilight of hedgebacks and hollows, ivy gropes through the damp, sweet-rotting humus, searching for something to climb. It soon finds a tree. If the tree is unhealthy, or lacks a light-restricting crown, then the ivy will take over. Eventually — maybe after decades — the tree will die, smothered, weighed down, exhausted. For years this made me resent ivy; the malicious plant seemed to be everywhere. Then, one afternoon I was caught in winter rain. The only shelter was under a tree choked by the woody climber. I wasn't alone. A group of Blackbirds and Song Thrushes had also claimed asylum. They were eating ivy berries — a massively nutritious food source, available in winter when all else is scarce. When the rain hardened, I pressed in closer to the ivy, and discovered a swathe of hibernating ladybirds. Evergreen ivy houses countless creatures. It also insulates its host tree against the elements. When the rain relented, I set off for home. Wrens were already gathering to roost in the ivy; their little songs ticked in the green depths like heartbeats. If ivy is death, it is also life. Van Gogh loved the plant for this paradox. The evergreen plant, the sunflower of the north, ivy covers his beloved brother's grave. For the great artist, ivy *was* death, but a gentle, natural passing, a death without fear, one sustained by hope.

We all know the old saying — in the midst of life, we are in death. Ivy flips this over and says — in the midst of death, we are in life.

We woke to find ice on the garden pond. Under a light snowfall, the frost was deep. The first frost of the year changes everything; it pushes open the back gate to winter so that you never know who might arrive. Later that day I was tending some saplings in the fields when I heard whistling. Half old-fashioned kettle, half haunting ghost, for a good few seconds I had no idea what it was, then I realised it was a flock of birds. Our Golden Plover were back. My heart rose. Breeding on the moors, the cold weather brings these birds to the lowlands. Every year a flock comes to us. Their return is one of the consolations of winter. Golden Plover congregations (their collective noun) have a distinctive, frankly unforgettable call, but they can be really difficult to spot. They'd passed close by, but I hadn't seen them. Jagging overhead like a school of herring, again and again they passed, their tight knit speed tricking my eye. At last they gave themselves away. *Pluvialis Apricaria* might leave their gold behind on the moors (their winter plumage is far drabber), but they bring with them the platinum flash of their underwings. And it was this sudden flash of bullion that gave them away. The wintry sun had struck them as they planed lowed over the horizon.

Summer visitors are usually expected; winter arrivals often come unexpected. When was the last time you were consoled by the surprise of a winter visitor?

The winter sun was setting when the Wood Pigeons lifted from the woods. A hundred, two hundred, three hundred of them. But instead of flying out over the acres of rapeseed in a chaos of clattering wings, as I have seen them do so many times before, they formed a single group drifting gently above the trees. Then, wheeling wildly, the flock turned in and out of itself, shrank to a thick, black density before bursting out into a looser formation again. It was a murmuration — the name we give to those huge, pulsing groups of birds, displaying unity before settling down to roost. Until now, I thought only Starlings behaved like this. All at once the Wood Pigeons took on the shape of a dolphin. Then a giant fish, before lapsing back into just a huge, fluctuating flight. To human eyes, Wood Pigeons are clumsy; almost comical. We talk of people being pigeon-toed or having a pigeon chest. Yet this winter flock was putting on a show of stunning grace. Beautiful as they may be, bird murmurations — whether Starling or Wood Pigeon — are a survival tactic. The twisting and turning is thought to mesmerise and confuse falcons. As much mathematical as artistic, the effect is caused by each bird flying as close to its neighbour as possible, instantly replicating any change of direction or speed. Thus the flock becomes a single unit.

If Wood Pigeons can become a dolphin just by sticking together, then what are we waiting for? Our possibilities are endless.

The gorse was in bloom at the top of the hill. Unable to resist a closer look, I vaulted the gate and climbed the steep slope of rough pasture to where the thorny bushes crowned the summit like the ramparts of some Iron Age hillfort. Yet dense, sharp, and prickly as the evergreen shrub was, its yellow flowers were as exquisite as any hothouse creation. A pair of Linnets chimed from deep within the spiny expanse of green and gold. Gorse blooms the year round, which probably explains why it was once a symbol of love — *when gorse goes out of season, kissing falls out of fashion* as the old saying goes. People also believed it kept evil away. In summer, chimneys were stuffed with its branches to keep the devil out. Scientists too have been susceptible to the plant's charms. Eighteenth-century botanist Carl Linnaeus fell to his knees and wept when he saw a heath of English gorse in full bloom. Smitten, he tried without success, to grow it in the too-cold Sweden. Gorse used to grow just about anywhere in Britain. An essential part of the rural economy, it was fuel, thatch and (properly prepared) animal fodder and bedding. After the gorse in the cottage chimney had done its job of keeping evil away, it was used to brush away the soot and tar.

Today I think I'll go for a walk and search for some gorse, or something similarly uncelebrated yet remarkable. Like Linnaeus, from time to time it does us good to get down on our knees before something truly great.

I only looked up for a second from my computer screen and there it was, in the cherry tree. Body, an eye-catching cinnamon-grey, wings tipped with yellow; but it was the crest that excited me. For a moment I thought I was looking at a parrot and then a jay before I realised what it really was: 'Waxwing!' I bellowed, my hands fumbling for the binoculars. The cover of my bird identification book had come dramatically alive. Waxwings, with their punk hairstyle, are rare but persistent visitors to the UK from Scandinavia and Northern Russia. When the rowan berries run short in their homelands, they head west to our gulf-stream-warmed parks and gardens. During their brief but intense sojourn, a wandering waxwing flock will gorge on one fruit tree after another until an entire neighbourhood has been stripped bare. Such feats of gluttony have sometimes led to allegations of drunkenness due to the fermenting state of the berries. Their winter presence is so ravenous and dramatic that it is referred to in birding circles as an irruption. When I finally got my binoculars trained, the rapacious easterner had gone. All morning I waited for the rest of the flock, but I had witnessed the strangest of phenomena: a solitary waxwing. Yet how exciting to begin a new year with a new species of bird; to see the outrider of a nomadic horde resting for a moment in our tree.

Beware, next time you look up from your computer screen, you might witness something little short of miraculous.

The gate creaked behind me as I entered the churchyard. My breath rose in great clouds. A rabbit scurried through the gravestones. I was heading for the holly tree — that dark green tower, lit with red berries. It was a rare frosty morning in this winter of wet and warm, and the ground crunched beneath my feet. Finding some holly leaves without barbs, I gathered them into my sack, careful not to dislodge their berries. Next, I headed for the yews, and watched by a Robin from its Christmas-card-perch in an apple tree, took a few boughs. They'll look great on the mantlepiece. They're likely to be the oldest thing not only in our house but the whole village. Human antiques can't compete with a yew bough; some churchyard yews are well over a millennium old. The Fortingall Yew in Perthshire is thought to be between 3,000 and 9,000 years old. I've been gathering our Christmas decorations here since we moved to the village many years ago, and over time little has changed except that now I know some of the names on the gravestones, some of them very well. The light was fading; time to head home. But first the Robin carolled me to where the ivy grew the thickest. I gathered it eagerly. The places where we bury our dead are those most full of life.

We live in decades, yews measure aeons. A visit to an old churchyard might be the nearest we get to time travelling.

I saw him again last night. Trotting down the village, tail feathering, he looked healthy, was obviously wintering well. In the glare of a suddenly passing car, his red fur gleamed. We first met one summer's twilight down the old cart track, and ever since then, I often meet my fox. I will never forget our first meeting. He crossed the lane directly in front of me, appearing and then disappearing again so seamlessly that the tip of his all-seeing nose and tail seemed to stitch a thread through the gathering dusk. Astonishing grace. I often encounter him at twilight. Truly, the proper prince of shadows. One winter day, ten years ago, I watched his father (or was it his grandfather?) outwit the local hunt. Belly slung to the ground, low and abject as a Somme soldier, he doubled back through the root field, which still held the scent of sheep, leaving the hounds baying at each other in frustration, and the horses at a standstill as though in imitation of the white limestone figure on the hill above nearby Kilburn. Most intimate perhaps, was our meeting when he was immersed in the consuming job of mating. Not noticing me, he was crouching under a fallen ash tree. Haggard with exhaustion, in his mouth he had three mice, gifts for his chosen vixen. Fellow provider, what resources your kind must own to have existed alongside us in all your wildness, on this crowded island. Ours is a shared inheritance: the sheer tenacity of life.

You can watch a hundred documentaries by David Attenborough, but what can compare to the breath-taking wildness of encountering a fox just a few yards from your front door?

The apple barrel stands in the corner of the garage. I switched on the torch and eased myself past the car and bikes towards it. Blowing off the cobwebs, I lifted the lid. The rich, fruity aroma rising to my nostrils sweetened the astringent smell of oil and old leaves clinging to the garage, and swept me back to the rosy months of summer and young autumn. Its glorious scent is always the apple barrel's first gift. After this comes the caress of the straw as you feel your way inside for the fruit, followed by the touch of the apple itself, solid, cold but reassuring. Then, of course, there's the first bite, which I took before I'd even got out of the garage. Despite the dusty darkness, I could taste the bright sunshine and gentle rains that had slowly plumped and ripened the fruit. Almost hear too, in the back teeth chomp, the bumble bees pollinating the spring blossom, the Blackbird singing from the boughs. Stored here since October, the apples were still fresh. They'd come from my nephew's old trees at the bottom of the village, and, like most traditional varieties, but unlike the modern supermarket breeds, were developed to both last *and* delight the taste buds. Closing my eyes, I took another bite. Here was a taste to lighten the darkest of January evenings.

Apples are simple yet perfect. A taste of eternity, the past lies in their slow growing, the present in their tangy flavour, the future resides in their seed.

I was walking through the falling snow when there was a plaintive tooting in the sky. A flock of swans was flying a hundred feet above. I watched them until they'd gone, then went on my way. I will never forget what happened next. An explosion of long neck and bill, a whirr of wings fanning air against my cheeks: a lone swan gliding low over me. Landing a few yards ahead she turned. The yellow beak and size revealed the largest of our three species: a Whooper Swan, one of the biggest flying birds on the planet. She tottered towards me. Spending summers in Iceland, they winter on our comparatively warmer shores. Many miles inland, her flock was lost, and this individual was even more lost, as the others continued without her. Lost *and* hungry. The bad weather must have forced her to break off and search for grass, stubble or sugar beet to munch. To differentiate them from the common Mute, Whoopers are also called the wild swan; their flocks have been tracked in the thin airs of 26,000 feet; this one was within my touch. She called out to me. Celtic mythology is rich with tales of humans and swans communicating. Now I know why. Our myth of swans singing an hour before dying most likely comes from the musical Whooper. Her wildness tamed by need, she gave another cry. The musical note held on the snow-stifled air: ravenous, raw, beautiful.

This happened nearly ten years ago, but every time I pass the same way, I remember it with a pristine clarity. That wild swan will accompany me forever. Nature offers its friendships without conditions.

Our Christmas tree lies discarded in the garden. Looking at it as I answer the phone, it seems hard to believe that it was only one short month ago that we trudged up through the torrential rain into the farmer's little plantation and, pointing at a fir sapling a few inches taller than my son, said: 'That one, please.' By common consent, this year's Christmas tree was our finest ever. Standing proudly in the corner of the lounge, it seemed to give off a calming, aqueous light; yet with the coming of the twelfth night, just like all the other temporary festive decorations, it had to go. I threw it onto the front lawn with the holly wreath, and that's where they've been ever since, discarded but not forsaken. The first visitor was a Blackbird attracted by the red berries of the wreath. Next on the scene was a wood mouse investigating the resinous tang. A Blue Tit arrived soon after, searching for the insects, which had colonised the little boughs during a brief warm period. Then finally, came the Wren. I first saw her about a fortnight ago, a tiny nut-brown bird hustling in and out of the still verdant needles. She was building a roosting pouch in the spiky safety.

That which the builders rejected, has become the cornerstone.

27

Who would have expected to find an orchard here? Throttled by dual carriageways and access roads, nigh on an acre of fruit trees stood within the shadow of the 'designer shopping outlet'. I paused at the gate. For a moment, in the half light of the midwinter afternoon, the old trees had the look of a resting herd of elephants: grey bark, thick and wrinkled as any pachyderm's skin; single branches lifted as though in trumpet; knotty holes twinkling like eyes. Despite the traffic roar and blare of the January sales, the moment I stepped into the orchard I felt a sense of calm. Some trees were dead or dying, but this was no graveyard; saplings had been planted, old trunks were protected from further rabbit damage, and someone had lovingly named each thriving tree. Hessle Pears, Keswick Codlin apples, Ponds seedling plums … unlike many of our fast disappearing 'lost' orchards, this one was clearly being cared for. Skirting fungi and vole runs, a little path threaded a way beneath the trees to an information board. I read how initially planted well over a hundred years ago, this had once been an orchard for the medical staff and patients of a psychiatric hospital. The hospital has long since been bulldozed to make way for the retail outlet, but this fragment of healing remains. I will come back in April when the blossom blazes.

Tortured by ever more cars and shopping centres, the world needs more orchards. Why not begin one today — go and plant a couple of fruit trees.

29

It seems a long time since we watched them arrive. Loose flock after flock chuntering over the autumn houses. We'd never seen so many Fieldfares before — would they never stop arriving? Today, they are an everyday sight in the little fields around the village. Having fled the iron of a Scandinavian winter, these large, grey-blue tinted thrushes bob continually through the waterlogged fields, feeding on berries and fruits, those secrets of the hedgerows. These birds are named for their constantly moving foraging habits, the Anglo-Saxon *feld-fere* means 'wayfarer through the fields'; as ever the English language finds its most intimate and poetic register in the humble. I love Fieldfares because of their faithfulness in times of cold adversity; how uplifting that a fellow creature should *choose* to share our much-maligned winters. I love them too because their name sounds the true note of my language. I love them also because they make us see the familiar with new eyes. With the help of Fieldfares, winter is no longer just the time to endure until spring returns; it is no longer a silence of loss when no twittering Swallows gladden the heart, nor Willow Warblers sing in the scrub. Winter becomes the season of Fieldfares, the time of visitors whose very name is a summons to pilgrimage. A time when we're called to search, like them, for sustenance. To wayfare through well-known fields, sodden as they are.

Do we see more by searching for the unfamiliar with our old eyes; or by gazing at the familiar through new eyes?

With the thaw, the beck swelled. Shaking the bank side alders and hurling flotsam downstream, the water ran in spate. I was watching a tree trunk bounce in mid current when I saw the Kingfisher on a branch. The contrast between bright feathers and turbid torrent was striking but what really caught my eye was the red-headed duck I suddenly spied bobbing under the Kingfisher's precarious perch. A moment of brilliant bafflement passed before I realised I was looking at a Goosander. It seemed impossible, but the streamlined duck was holding her own against the flood. The beautifully ginger-headed Goosander first arrived in the UK in 1871; starting in Scotland, they spread south, crossing the border in 1970. An intriguing species, they display many un-duck-like characteristics. Not only do they nest in trees, growl when disturbed, and carry ducklings on their back, but they also have a serrated beak. This sawbill allows them to devour young salmon and trout. To catch these fish, the Goosanders collaborate. Often operating in cooperatives, one member drives the quarry to the others. Perhaps it's this skill that has led them to spread, and could it also be this I was observing now, as the Goosander fought to keep under the Kingfisher? With food scarce, were the two species cooperating, the duck driving the fish to the waiting beak, which they would then share?

We're taught that the world is one big competition; but the more I look, the more I see cooperation.

One of these days I'll compile a list of the fascinating things I've seen in car parks. Last weekend, on the road with my ceilidh band, we pulled into a market town for a fry-up. Leafless with winter, tall lime trees towered over the parked vehicles. Taking in a deep breath of cold air, we noticed a snag of shaggy greenery near the top of one of the limes. The leaves of this thick, bushy growth dandled down like seaweed. Being northerners none of us had seen wild mistletoe growing before — it thrives most abundantly in the Welsh borders and cider counties of the South West — but we knew it couldn't be anything else. What was it doing in a Yorkshire car park? Having been a largely sedentary plant for centuries, lately mistletoe has been on the move. And it's all due to the changing habits of a little warbler with a big voice, the Blackcap. Once migrant, Blackcaps have begun overwintering in Britain, during which time they indulge their passion for mistletoe berries. Feasting on the fruit, the song birds then fly to other trees and wipe their beaks clean of the sticky, white flesh. The dislodged seeds germinate, setting up new colonies. Favouring orchards and the open aspect of non-woodlands, mistletoe will find a tree-fringed car park to be home from home.

Come and travel in the slow, winding back lanes of nature. Gradually head north in the company of mistletoe and its travelling companion, the Blackcap.

'Aye,' the woman said, joining me at the gate. 'She's the last of her kind. Time was every village round here had its winter donkey.' I watched as the patient animal slowly approached. When she was within reach, I stroked her. The withers of her thick winter coat were soft and warm, and enticed a flurry of pats. Her long, intelligent ears thanked me. Donkeys do a lot of talking with their ears. Nostrils sending up a light steam in the frost, her nose gently read me as she stared with those probing eyes. 'Scarborough, Whitby, Filey,' the woman continued. 'Used to be full of donkeys, and of course there had to be somewhere for them to go come winter. This was their holidays.' As though in memory of the golden shore of summer, the donkey's dainty hooves lightly pawed the frozen ground. Along with dogs, what other animals are so entwined with humanity as the ass? Domesticated for 5,000 years, they're pictured carrying wheat in ancient Egyptian art; in the Bayeux tapestry they plough the land. What childhood is complete without a donkey ride? Recorded as living well into their fifties, perhaps this one once bore me over wet sands on a far-off August day in Blackpool. Parting at last, I was only a few yards down the road when a bray summoned me back.

The days of childhood are short, but last forever.

After the shrinking of the snow, a long tongue of ice lingered on the field. It was as we were playing an improvised game of curling along this frozen chute (piece of wood as the jack, nearest sliding stone wins) that my son made the discovery. The moment he'd dredged up the hand-sized stone from the glutinous mud for his turn, we knew he'd found something special. The light-coloured rock seemed to glint in the crisp, midwinter, noon sun. On closer inspection, we saw that it was covered in blue-ish decorations. Our ice game forgotten, we washed it in a stream of ice-melt. The patterns became more pronounced. Tadpole like squiggles, rows of small teeth, peering eyes. Were we looking at a fossil or something from the human epoch? There certainly seemed to be manual artistry behind the markings, yet we know that the hand of time also appears to work by design. Millions of years old or a thousand? The wriggling soup of a long-gone aeon caught in a second of stone, or the product of the Vikings who had their kingdom in these parts? Either way, it seemed miraculous. On a day of rapidly melting ice, during a scratch game shared by father and son, we, creatures of an eye blink, had found something with such longevity. In turn, we weighed the stone in the scales of our hands as though reckoning gold.

We live in a world where even the stones in the field hold a million mysteries, but these are as nothing to the epic enigma of our loved ones.

It's that time of the year again. The winter seems endless; the days appear locked into a trance of cold winds, semolina skies and cheerless suns. Yet despite this, nominations for the George Orwell prize for Early Signs of Spring are already being taken. Here are a few of my suggestions. The ever-faithful hawthorn. At first glance February hawthorns seem utterly lifeless, but a suddenly sunny day will reveal daubs of red in the swelling bud. These will fan into the first flames of spring. Then there's the ivy. Grey and nondescript, the ivy berries, ripening now, are a vital part of nature's late winter/early spring economy, providing nourishment for birds and mice just when the larder is empty. An even more unobtrusive candidate for the award is the aptly named spring usher moth. Delicately dabbled as the oak bark which fed their larvae, the spring usher moth will start taking to the air any day now. Although it will fly past few flowers, everywhere it'll see the lichens in bloom. Like little suns of Mediterranean yellow, the golden lichens, glowing on trees, stones and even roof tiles, turn our lanes into subjects fit for the brush of a Van Gogh. An outsider for the prize are the raucous Rooks. They've just started their lengthy negotiations over the flotsam of twigs lodged in the top of the beeches — March's nests.

What compares to the power of a winter sun?

The winds rose in the night. All morning, they strengthened. By afternoon, when I headed out for my walk, the trees were tossing and waving. I kept being blown from the path. Only the Herring Gulls seemed able to ride the gale; their white, arched wings barely rippling in the gusts. I was near the caravan site when I glimpsed a black shape passing high overhead. Half mini-dragon, half pterodactyl, its oddness brought me to a halt. This was no gull. It could only be a cormorant. A new species in the area! I ran after it through the caravan site, deserted at this time of year, and arrived at the lily pond just as the cormorant was landing in the water. Once a coastal species, these goose-sized birds are now spreading inland. Had this one been blown here on the wind and taken a liking to fat carp nosing under the lily pads? Then I saw more of the birds. Three of them sat in a bare winter willow with their wings hanging out to dry in the classic fashion. Their wonderful blackness shone like fertile soil freshly ploughed. It was due to this rich darkness that Cormorants were also once known as *sea crows* and *coal geese*. Perched in the tree, wings wide, white throats glinting, it was easy to see why they were also known as *parsons*.

Next time there's a windy day, why not go outside and see if you can catch what the world is throwing your way?

You know the kind of day — a raw wind and a February sun that stings your eyes without warming your face. I was on the bridleway's most exposed point when the hare surprised me. Concealed in the long grass beside the path, it suddenly rose on long legs, and lumbered away through the winter wheat. Head low, body cambered, its amber eyes and black-tipped ears seemed larger than ever. Giving a sudden, stunning leap, the hare's stretched length of golden fur and sinew shone in the sharp clarity of the late winter light. I never see a hare without being deeply touched. I'm not the only one. In fact, a hare saved the life of one of the greatest poets and hymn writers of the eighteenth century. William Cowper, losing his reason, was committed to a lunatic asylum. He'd tried suicide at least three times, and a fourth attempt seemed likely when an orphaned leveret was brought to him. The poet immediately set about nursing the animal and building it a pen. When the locals heard how the tender madman loved his new charge, fed it most assiduously, the poet was inundated with orphaned hares. He took them in. In return, they helped him regain his sanity, and he began writing again. For Cowper, a hare's ears were as expressive as poetry, its amber eyes the most moving of metaphors.

Nature is a sonnet writer, scientist and therapist. A provider of poetry, mysteries and antidotes to despair — free at the point of use.

We had thought the long silence was nearly over. All winter the rich song of the earth had withered to a meagre music: Blackbirds sifting the leaf mould, the creaking of frost-bound ash trees and the wind improvising grimly on the same few cheerless tunes in the blackthorn brake. But recently this freezing of sound has been thawing at the edges, as titmice and thrushes test the weight of the silence. Then last night, snow came. We drew the curtains back on a smothering, unequivocal, searing stillness. With hats, mittens and scarves we braved a hush so absolute as to be startling. How could something so light weigh so heavily? The sledge merely whispered as we ran over the great white-over of the village cricket field on which the derelict pavilion had been transfigured into the lodge of a winter palace. Our laughter travelled no more than a few yards. We were in the silent heart of winter. The stillness-gatherer, snow, effaces us all; shows us as creatures whose tracks in this world are soon covered by the flurries of mortality. But it also allows us to hear a kindly hush, where all ugliness is made beautiful, all mistakes erased and scars healed — like the fading of footsteps taken in the wrong direction. Trudging our way home, we turned to look where we had played. Already our prints were being covered by a fresh fall.

Snow falls like forgiveness; forgiveness falls like snow.

Every year is different. This winter belongs not to the Siskins and Tree Sparrows of last year, but to the Blackbirds, Chaffinches and a Great-spotted Woodpecker that grins as he descends the greasy pole of the cherry tree. The bird table is a corner of the world of which I can never tire. In the words of the broken poet Theodore Roethke, it's a place to recover your tenderness by long-looking. As well as the faithful visitors, the bird table also has its exhilarating one-offs. Like the strangers who arrived this morning, when the Blackbirds were eating the halved apples. Up close, the beauty of a Redwing is breath-taking. Its light eye stripe is a single, delicate brushstroke, its flanks and underwings flash the rich russet of the autumn woods over which they flew to us when first arriving from Scandinavia. One of the Redwing's other names is Swine-pipe, because of the resemblance its soft, winter call bears to the pipes that swineherds once played to summon their pigs from out of the woods. As we listened to the Swine-pipes arriving in the garden, whistling plaintively over their feeding fields, the land suddenly seemed full of memory. Musical swineherds have been silent for centuries, but here were their echoes. One of the special gifts of the bird table is to restore an inheritance largely lost since the industrial revolution: our casual, day to day comradeship with animals. We need such intimacy to remind us that the heart of life beats not to the rhythm of electronic bleeps, nor the computer keyboard, but to the sudden flurry of a bird's wings. Our profoundest aspiration is for a flight that can take us far, far beyond the chair-bound reaches of the internet.

*

If winter ever feels endless and dire, may I prescribe a bird table? A simple set of feeders will give you endless entertainment and introduce you to neighbours you may never have dreamt of having.

The lambs' tails wagged in the wind. Not the woolly variety, but the catkins on the hazel tree. The rest of the wood edge was drab and colourless, but the hazel was a riot of dangling, shimmering, yellow tassels. Is there a more striking sight that spring is at last on its way? The catkins are the tree's male flowers; the female flowers are far less conspicuous, yet just as vivid. Growing on the same tree, you have to really search for them. I found one at last — a carmine wisp, right on the tip of a bud. Not as showy as the male perhaps, but come autumn this will be the nut. Both male and female flowers are wind pollinated; just as well, few insects were flying on this raw, February afternoon. Halfway between a shrub and a tree, if left to themselves hazels have a lifespan similar to our own; if coppiced, they can live for two centuries. Extremely pliable, hazel wood was used for fencing, cottage furniture and thatching spars, but it was for its tasty, nutritious nut that the tree was most highly prized. Hazels were considered to have more than mere practical gifts however. In Gaelic culture, nine hazel trees grew round the well of wisdom. When their nuts fell into the water, a salmon gobbled them down, and gained the wisdom of the entire world.

Maybe wisdom is not a quarry, a prize to be stalked and secured, nor a star to be reached, but a mind open enough to catch whatever falls its way.

'Chacker-chacker-chack' rings out over the houses: a Magpie sailing overhead, long bottle green tail fluttering, stick in beak. If Disney held auditions for the role of Spring, it's unlikely they'd choose a Magpie. With its death rattle call and penchant for egg stealing, Magpies are often seen as the bird world's boot boys. No accident that Rossini cast the species in his *The Thieving Magpie*, a larcenous role reprised in Hergé's *Tintin and the Castafiori Emerald*. With a popular tag like 'one for sorrow', Magpies are always going to have trouble winning public affection and yet despite this, they do indeed constitute one of our most welcome heralds of spring. Right now, just as stamina and hope are at their lowest, these multicoloured master builders are starting work on their nests. These days you see them passing overhead everywhere, high as the cranes above a building site, beaks bearing construction materials. It'll take them weeks, but when finished the Magpie nest is the most secure. Such house-building prowess must have been behind the English folk tale in which all the other birds are taught nest building by the Magpie. Inspired by the lesson and impatient to start their own, one by one the birds leave the demonstration, none stay to the end and so none learn the Magpie's chief wisdom: a dome of thorny twigs is the best line of defence.

The much-maligned Magpie's nest building is one of spring's ways of whispering its own name.

I paused for a while beneath the alder that grows by the beck. For months it has been a sombre even austere sculpture of grey and brown. But now, at the end of winter, it seemed to glint in my eye. When I looked more closely I saw that the whole tree was tinged with purple. The catkins were in bloom. Trees of river, stream and marsh, alders maintain our waterways; their roots not only prevent bank erosion but also provide shelter for fish. Their quickly decaying leaves create just the right nutrients for the larvae of caddis flies and other staples of the riparian food chain. Its white wood bleeds to red on being sawn, and since it does not rot under water is ideal for the construction of waterside buildings: virtually the whole of Venice is underpinned by alder piles. In our own, supposedly high-tech era, alders are just as useful. The nodules of their roots fix nitrogen, helping to clean, reclaim and once again make fertile sites degraded by industry or intensive agriculture. Small wonder that the alder figures large in mythology; in fact, it was considered to be sacred in the faery world, the dye from its catkins making faeries invisible, an aid to adventure which Robin Hood himself was said to use whilst evading the law. I tarried a little longer. A breeze whispered through the alder, and its rustling purple seemed to crackle under the foot of departing winter.

One of winter's greatest gifts is to reward our faithfulness. Have you shivered and yearned for colour through the short days of winter? Then yours is the joy of the green leaf, the caress of the kinder breeze; the slow, healing lengthening of light.

Spring

Bringing the washing in from the line, we laid it over the bed. A buzzing began. A pyjama top moved slightly. The buzz grew louder. Then a bee popped out from the pyjama jacket pocket. It was a buff-tailed bumble bee queen, our largest bee and the first to emerge from hibernation in spring. She must have crawled into the clothing to get warm. Dragging herself onto the pillow, she paused a moment as though to gather all her energy. As she rose from the pillow, her vigour seemed to shake the whole room. I hurried to the window and threw it open. Bumble bees rarely sting but I didn't want her to hurt herself. With the power of a thrown stone, she hurled herself through the open window and out into the world. Her job was to find a suitable hole as soon as possible. An old mouse or vole nest in a dry bank would be perfect. Here she'll lay half a dozen or so eggs, cocooned in nectar and wax. Hatching in a few days, these will be the first workers of the colony, which may grow to house up to 150 bees. And so, spring starts. We stood for a long time at the window after the queen had gone. When Noah saw the dove, he knew all was well. I felt the same way.

They were wrong. There are infinitely more wonders of the world than just seven. For me, the greatest is a bumble bee waking in spring.

Our cherry plum tree is in blossom. All at once its brittle twigs are lit with white. Sparrows plunge in and out of the gently scented branches like children playing in a fountain. A blackbird sings from the very top – a single silhouette in the brilliance. The bloom is so bright that you can see the tree from halfway down the village. At twilight, it lights up the gathering darkness like a shooting star; through the night, it is a moon orbiting the garden. At dawn it blazes like a flare. Sometimes, I just stand at the window watching. Nobody asked this tree to bloom, nobody built it, wired it or designed it; no one even planted it, yet here it is, impossibly beautiful. And these shining cascades of early spring blossom are only the beginning of the tree's talents. It spends from now 'til August singing. Or at least the bees in the blossom do, after which the melody is taken up by the Goldfinches, which nest in the very fingertips of the tree and fill our garden with their tinkling chimes until late summer. Then of course there's the fruit that comes: purple, juicy and scrumptious. Travel the world and I might never meet with a finer sight, than the tree always waiting for me at the bottom of the garden.

If you were only allowed one tree, what would it be? What's your 'desert island' tree?

The sun came out and I closed my eyes. For the first time in months I felt something akin to warmth on my face. In the next field, a Skylark rose higher and higher pouring out its song. Bathing in the notes of the Skylark's melody, I carried on along the soggy by-way. The snowdrops were at their height — the latest and finest showing of them I can remember. Pouring down muddy hollows or scattered above ditches, I love the way these little white flowers always grow in scruffy corners, as if they have been swept there by some serendipitous broom to form an example of the beauty of haphazardry. Seen as symbols of hope and purity, in the Middle Ages snowdrops were dedicated to the Virgin Mary. It's impossible to enjoy their scent without kneeling and stooping low enough to kiss the soft earth. Having done so, I gently lifted one of the white bells and breathed in the gentle fragrance. Climbing back to my feet, the path took me through the village where Jackdaws were pairing up on their ancestral chimney pots, and the Greenfinches were bright as canaries. Soon these cottage gardens will be filled with the colour of countless blooms and the sound of bees; today they held just the dark earth and its muddy but dependable promise of beauty; yet will anything be as joyful as these first white flowers straggling on the by-way?

*

Snowdrops belong to that select group of plants — the ones everyone recognises. Each year they ask us — do you accept our gifts?

I wasn't the only one up early. As I biked through the back lanes, with the dawn mist just lifting, the Curlew's cry sounded out. There's nothing like the sound of a Curlew. The haunting lilt of notes blew through the bare, early spring fields like a breeze from the wilderness. Impossible not to stop when you hear a Curlew. I pulled up, got off my bike, and leaning against a gate, listened. The field seemed full of curlews, there were at least a dozen. They'd just arrived here from the coast where they overwinter. Even as I stood there, the last of the mist melted, and the birds were revealed in all their breeding finery. Their grey-brown feathers seemed to glow, their white back flashed like lightning. The music poured from their huge, slender, tender beaks like a reel from a fiddler's bow. Proportionately, Curlews must have the longest bill of any European bird; surely no other species has the grace of this musical beak; that flowing, upside down parabola: more like a harp's curved column than a fiddler's bow. The female Curlew has the longer bill. I can't agree with William Butler Yeats, who reprimands the Curlew for having a call that brings back painful memories. For me the evocative call brings to mind what is to come rather than what has been. I can never hear a Curlew without feeling forgiven.

Humans evolved to the sound of birdsong; our ear is drawn to its depths. This is why we fathom with the heart so many things that we can never comprehend with the head.

If I were a king I would willingly give up my domains and dominions for the tawny mining bee. What's a potentate's throne beside the small tangle of back garden on which I encountered this spring bee last week? Just emerged from hibernation, it lay in the sun on the long grass. Gradually warming, it looked so new that it made the whole world seem freshly created. Tawny is too thin a word. After a long winter of sere and ashen grey, the tawny mining bee is a sudden, bright brush splashing colour wherever it flies. Part fiery ginger, part fox, part midnight black, this bee burns brilliantly, lighting the darkest heart. Nesting underground, it is also known as the lawn bee for its habit of rearing its colonies in gardens. Look out for little volcanoes of soil amongst the daisies. Its ability to granulate soil so finely not only reminds us that the tawny miner is a member of the sand bee family, but that we are in the presence of an artist. It won't sting, so we can still pad around the dandelions in bare feet. On the wing from March to June, these common solitary bees love to feed on the fruit trees of the season. If I were a king I would abdicate my authority, my every palace for a single tawny mining bee.

Somehow, we humans instinctively recognise the true currency of the world. And nothing in a palace or at the command of a billionaire's credit card, can match the incomparable riches of watching a tawny mining bee.

Our old friend the north wind doth blow. We're well into March, but spring seems to have run away. This afternoon, toiling into bitter gusts, I was about to call it a day and head for home, when I saw the Treecreeper. There were two of them in the alders. Leaving the footpath for a closer look, I found myself stepping back into spring — the alders grew in the lee of the woods and were sheltered from the wind. Protected from the strickening wind-chill factor, the air temperature soared. Enjoying the relative warmth, I watched the Treecreepers mounting the alder trunk. They always go up trees, never down, climbing the trunk in tight, ascending feeding spirals. This habit has shaped the very way they look. Their mottled brown and white plumage is speckled, shaded and shaped to perfectly camouflage them picking their way up a tree trunk. With this sleight of hand, the Treecreeper is usually well hidden from predators, such as Great-spotted Woodpeckers, red squirrels and stoats. Almost entirely insectivorous, Treecreepers will also munch the occasional pine or alder seed on days when nothing else is to be found. They mount each tree by hopping up with their feet together, like abseilers in reverse. A stiff tail acts like a crampon. It's been estimated that every day each tiny bird climbs higher than any mountain in the UK.

The smallest are the mightiest — that's just the way things are.

Hail storms. Snow. North winds turning umbrellas inside out. Yet another frigid spring. Yesterday, the Swallows, having just arrived, gathered in confusion on the telephone wires. A slow spring has *some* benefits though. The flowers are lasting longer, and not just daffodils. This morning, when the weather suddenly turned sunny and calmer, I went for a walk along the beck and found the butterbur still in bloom. Butterbur is one of our first flowers to blossom. In looks, halfway between a toadstool and rhubarb, the spikey, fleshy pink flowers of butterbur have an unconventional beauty. Bees love their early nectar; in the past, hives would be placed to overwinter in clumps of the plant, waiting for their first flower in March. It's not just their flowers that are remarkable, but their leaves, which come out after the plant blooms. If you've ever walked along a beck, you'll have seen their huge, umbrella leaves. Large enough to use as rain hats in summer downpours, they can also double up as parasols in heatwaves — their long stalks serve as useful handles. Current research is examining how extracts of the plant might help combat migraine headaches. Our forebears used them to store butter, hence their name. In the days before refrigerators, the leaves kept the food cool and fresh.

A useful poetry — habits of the past are often preserved in the names of our flora and fauna.

We call it Bullfinch Boulevard because more often than not when strolling this way, you'll encounter a party of browsing Bullfinches. It was as we walked down this avenue of rough pasture, lined on one side by a belt of downy birch underlain with blackthorn, and on the other by a wide ditch overhung with hawthorn, that we first heard the Bullfinch's remarkable love song. So soft that it seemed nothing more than the barely audible rising of sap, or the tuneful creaking of branches, we only realised that it was a bird when we got directly beneath the serenader's branch and looked up to see the Bullfinch above us. He was wearing his crimson cape and black matador's hat. Crooning tenderly, he sat amongst the dangling, downy birch catkins. The Bullfinch sings as gracefully as he picks fruit buds, and not for territory or power but simply for his mate to whom he is attached all his life. In the past, this tremendous singing ability often doomed the Bullfinch to a cage. Kept in captivity, the birds could be taught folk melodies; Queen Victoria and the Russian Tsar being amongst the gaolers. There were even professional Bullfinch song teachers. Contemporary accounts state that Chopin's tune *Thou art so like a flower* could often be heard in the Bullfinch markets. How wonderful then to stroll down the Boulevard of *free* Bullfinches and hear their tender song of love and liberty.

*

A bird in a cage sets all heaven in a rage. Every living being should be free. Who can we help set free?

At last the spring flowers are blooming. The first I've noticed this year are the lesser celandines. For weeks I've been watching their heart-shaped leaves growing gradually glossier, until yesterday their bright yellow flowers suddenly burst into life. Members of the buttercup family, lesser celandines are woodland plants so if you're lucky enough to have them in your garden, chances are your lawn used to be part of an ancient wood. They'll flourish too on damp waste ground, path edges and under hedges. William Wordsworth treasured these little spring flowers above all others. To him they were more fascinating and beautiful than the stars. He loved them for their humility and democracy too — they grow where they must, more likely by a cottage door than in a king's courtyard. He also liked the almost human way they shrink from cold rainy weather, by folding their flowers. When Wordsworth died, celandines were carved on the great poet's tomb, but by mistake the flowers depicted were greater celandines, very different from the springtime lesser celandines. In *The Lion, the Witch and the Wardrobe,* one of the signs of Aslan's coming is the sudden constellation of lesser celandines growing in a glade of silver birch trees. Less poetic perhaps is the fact that this plant was used to treat piles, hence its alternative name of pilewort.

Spring brings the stars right to our feet. Wildflowers too grow in constellations.

I love walking beneath the scots pines where the Rooks nest. A busy road runs close by, but when you pass under the trees you're lifted up and immersed in the soundworld of these glossy, purple-black members of the crow family. This morning, before catching my train, I stood beneath the pines for half an hour just listening. Rooks are highly talkative, and I could hear not only the famous, raucous 'craaa', one of my favourite noises of early spring, but also, during gaps in the traffic, a far quieter, curiously gentle, click-clacking sound, almost like the kind of gurgling humans might make to a baby. There's more to Rook music than all that deafening cawing! I counted thirty nests in the trees. They've been here for as long as I can remember, which is just as well, since long term rookeries are considered a sign of good luck. In *David Copperfield*, Charles Dickens' novel inspired by his own disastrous childhood, the desertion of the rookery in the trees growing round his native home, is a sign of impending disaster. Other superstitions that used to surround the bird are their nests. If they build them low in a tree it's said that the summer will be cold and wet, if they build them high, then the year will be good. Thankfully, my Rooks' nests were right at the top of the pines.

Of all the astonishing gifts of spring, not least the tender crooning of the Rooks.

I can ask for no more. Today on my favourite walk, I met a Yellowhammer in a hawthorn. Of course, with their citrus yellow heads and russet bodies, every encounter with these colourful members of the bunting family is special, but to see one in this particular tree moved me deeply. When I first started walking this way years ago, there were no trees, just the ecological desert of a massive, chemically-farmed arable field. And of course, without trees there were few insects and birds. It felt like a lonely place to walk. That's why I started planting saplings along the footpath. This hawthorn was one of my first. Against all the odds (drift from the crop sprayer, winds gusting through the treeless fields, hungry deer and the annual mechanical flail cutting back the path), the tree survived, but didn't flourish. Ten years on, it was no taller than a human child starting school. Then, two Mays ago, it suddenly came into bloom. Today as I passed by, it was a vortex of green thorn and bridal bloom, topped with a Yellowhammer. Head a vivid blob of Van Gogh yellow, the bird was singing with gusto — defending a breeding territory? If so, then its mate would be on a nest under the hawthorn itself, or close by under one of my other trees. Life had returned.

I find it impossible to spend time with a tree without being filled with hope.

The newt rose from the depths of the garden pond like a cosmonaut drifting weightlessly through space. Toes spread, tail gently steering, it glided into a dark cluster of watercress. Freshly out of its woodpile hibernaculum, the male smooth newt (Lissotriton vulgaris) was in breeding fettle. Dark spots dappled the length of his 10cm body, a serrated crest ran along his back, his terracotta-coloured belly was almost orange. The newt hadn't been gone from view for long when there was a flurry of activity in the starwort. A female newt (no crest) was surrounded by three males. Sandwiching the female, the males were thrashing about and twirling their tails. This is the famous 'newt dance', a common sight in the breeding season, during which time this usually languid amphibian becomes an extravagant raver. Such behaviour, of course, led to the famous, if rather indecorous phrase about states of inebriation. And the show wasn't over yet. For a few moments I thought that it had started to rain, but the pond wasn't puckering with water drops, rather there were more female newts, all shooting up to collect floating spermatophore capsules. One after the other, with the grace of brown trout, they darted to the surface before flashing back into the mini depths. Eggs now fertilised, the females began to lay, wrapping their spawn tenderly in the watercress.

In spring, we're all dancers.

Is there anyone still alive who can remember the heyday of the cowslip? Once as common as garden daisies, these gregarious yellow flowers used to chatter their way across the countryside in such profusion that many Anglican churches celebrated 'cowslip Sunday'. A number of hymns were even written to celebrate this sociable spring bloom. In late April and May, Eastenders would descend on the fields of Essex and carry great armloads home to freshen and brighten their city lives. Going back further in time, every cottage would have its bottles of cowslip wine and cowslip tea. These days, well when did you last see a single wild cowslip, let alone a pride of them painting a field gold? People talk of the loss of the great buffalo herds and the shrinking rainforests, but doesn't the disappearance of the British cowslip belong in that hall of shame? How can we lecture other countries on their environmental records when we can't find space for these spring delights? Consequently, I was amazed last week, travelling east of Leeds, to see miles (literally) of cowslips. The motorway embankment rose from the roaring froth of carbon dioxide and pollution particulates, in a vast, cleansing lemon wave. Shaking and nodding in the AI(M) wind, the cowslips wandered up and down the motorway embankment as if it were some dell in 1826.

The world is full of tiny resurrections in the unlikeliest of places.

Last night I dreamt I was back in the house where I grew up. All the old companions were there: the creak on the stair, the cat on my bed, the tawny owls calling from the oaks on the scaur rising above the river and the birch tree that dominated our back yard. How many hours did I spend staring at that tree as a boy? There was always something different to see. Goldfinches, woodpeckers, Starlings and Linnets. In middle age now, I'm still yet to see a couple-colour as ravishing as the smoky head and red crest of the Linnets that used to chime in those white branches. In my dream I could hear the never-ending, always shunting of the trains; we lived above the railways marshalling yards to the north of Carlisle, a place of milch cattle, goods trains and acres of former railway sidings slowly turning into heath and woods. But it was the river I was gladdest to meet again. Recently, the River Eden has become famous as a trespasser, flooding the streets of Carlisle; to us it was always a gentle companion. It meanders through my childhood, carrying half of the soft waters of Cumbria, and often us too — days upon days we swam in it with the eels and Kingfishers, and the waterweed dandling dreamily below us.

We aren't rooted in our childhoods, but it's where we've been blown from, like dandelion seeds.

There's only going to be one winner here and it doesn't look like being me. I've tried various bars, cages, and chains but my adversary has proved more than equal. Each time I have tried to up the ante and think I've produced something critter-proof, the little grey squirrel comes sauntering over the lawn and after a brief moment of hesitation proceeds to pour scorn on my efforts. I tried nailing a broom handle high across the cherry tree and dangling the bird feeder from a three-foot chain but I soon saw that the little fellow had somehow managed to get on top of the feeder and was helping itself in royal style. And neither did it avail anything when I increased the length of the chain to five feet. The extra length merely seemed to add flavour to the challenge. I don't know what the neighbours make of such tree ornaments but I know that our long-tailed visitors thrive on them, and all we can do is to admire their ingenuity. It's believed that the entire British population of grey squirrels can be traced to 10 intrepid individuals brought to Woburn Abbey in 1890. Ecologists may dislike some of the grey squirrel's more anti-social characteristics but what other animal can dispense hubris to *homo sapiens'* self-appointed supremacy with such mischievous nonchalance?

*

Sometimes you just have to accept that you're not going to win, and admire the victor!

The toad was waiting at the front door. Warty dry skin, golden-eyed, the amphibian crawled inside, and headed for the lounge. We've had toads in the house before, (carried in on firewood), but never such a determined guest. Scooped into a box, the toad gaped at me, and swelled. Toads swell for the serious matter of self-defence, hoping to shock an otter into dropping them perhaps, but to the human eye it seems comic. In fact, if you spend any time close to a toad you'll see how our word buffoon is rooted in the toad's Latin name of *bufo bufo*. Easy to see too how Kenneth Grahame got his inspiration for his boastful Toad of Toad Hall. Yet, as with all nature (humans included), toads are quietly heroic. At this time of year with breeding in full swing, they travel huge distances to return to their spawning grounds. Some journeys are a mile and a half, with around fifty metres being travelled in a night. That's an Odyssey for such a small, lumbering animal, and every inch must be crawled, because unlike the frog, the common toad doesn't jump. These treks are fraught with obstacles and danger. Walls can be climbed by the determined animals, but roads are not so easy. It's estimated that 20 tonnes of migrating toads die annually on UK roads. Against all the odds, still they come.

If you want to meet a toad (or frog or newt) then dig a pond in your garden. And never use weed killer. *You'll soon be meeting these heroes for yourself.*

Walking down the old cart lane and then on to the fields, I was paying so little attention to the world that I almost stepped on one of its miracles. What else could you call the Yellow Wagtail? Yes, other birds migrate across continents to get here too, but then they're built for journeying. The Swallow, Swift and Arctic Tern are not only a perfection of aerodynamics, but also, they live most of the year on the wing, virtually their entire lives in the case of the Swift. In contrast, their fellow globetrotter, the Yellow Wagtail spends the bulk of its life walking on the ground. Hunkering down, I watched the little bird pottering around me. That long fluttering tail and dancer's step, which makes it able to dart under cattle hooves to snatch insects, can surely only be a hindrance in crossing oceans? Built for flying in field-sized undulations, having just arrived from West Africa no wonder he's so exhausted that he can't even be bothered to get out of the way of the human clodhopper. A voyage akin to you or me crossing open seas in a public-park rowing boat. At last the new arrival wandered away to be joined by a Pied Wagtail. The black and white plumage of the annual resident deepens the gold of the light-coloured summer visitor so that the true miracle is revealed: Africa has arrived.

For nearly twenty years now I've barely travelled anywhere. This is what I've learnt: to see the world, stay in the same place. Like the Yellow Wagtails, it will come to you in its own time.

This year the primroses are more magnificent than ever. An exhibition of sun-tones, in the colony growing on the verge of the road at the bottom of our village some individuals are the most muted of creams, whereas others are so bright that they seem to sparkle like neon lamps in the grass. There is something utterly charming about the way primroses grow in scatters; as though they have rolled in from somewhere and taken root only the night before they bloom. But in fact, they are remarkably stationary, individual plants living for up to 25 years in the same inch of earth. Their seed diffusion is slow, mobility restricted to the grinding locomotive of an ant-line or the jolting of raindrops. Ironically, one of their best methods of spreading was in the days when children picked them en masse. There is evidence that the increasing and opening up of public footpaths is helping them to spread again. An emblem of spring, primroses have always had a special place at the heart of folklore. In many parts of the country they were made into garlands and hung from front doors. Never removed when they died, they were left to wither on the wood: a reminder of the aching brevity of beauty. Woodcutters also used them; when boiled in lard, they helped heal their cuts. And they are still healing us today. Even the car becomes a pleasant place when we can stop at the primrose verge.

Unlike the creations of hothouses and horticulture, primroses are meant to be mauled, stood on, picked and scattered. They don't stand on ceremony.

As I was making a cup of tea in the kitchen, I heard a single, sharp, decidedly imperious rap on the back door. Having scalded my teabag, I went to answer it. A peacock stood on the doorstep. Bold as brass, it knocked again, its bill striking the glass with alarming power, before wandering off. I've often heard the peacocks calling from the caravan park over in the next village but it's the first time one has ever crossed the fields to us. Returning to work, five minutes later I received a phone call. 'Did you know there's a peacock on your roof?' A neighbour asks. 'I think it's come down now,' I replied as the bird jumped down past my window, its dazzling azure neck flashing in the sun, the eyes of its long tail interrogating me. As well as being stunningly beautiful, in the wild, peacocks, the national bird of India, can be pretty formidable, eating small mammals, reptiles and snakes. In this country their domestication is often only skin deep, and they can inflict damage on cars, flower beds, and even back doors. So serious is this that local government advice — should one enter your garden — warns you never to feed one. *If you encourage a stray bird to stay on your land you may be legally considered its owner and liable to any damage it causes.* From the safety of my window I watched the exotic miscreant begin to dig up my young cabbages ....

What's your 'national bird' of spring?

We all know that we have to welcome strangers because, who knows, we might be entertaining angels, but no one mentioned archangels. Yet that's exactly what I was asked to do today. There's a low wall between us and our neighbour. In the wall is a gap for hedgehogs. Yesterday I was looking at the gap and saw, not a hedgehog, but some yellow flowers I'd never seen before. They were archangels, or to give them their full name, yellow archangels. I glanced over the wall; my neighbour's herbaceous border had been overtaken by these wild flowers, and now they were spreading into ours. Members of the mint family, yellow archangels are a 'greenwood indicator'; in other words, where they grow was once, relatively recently, ancient woodland. Our ordinary, even humble garden was once that arcadia, ancient woodland. As well as being travellers from the past, yellow archangels often perform a double act with bluebells, soaring into bloom just as the bluebells are fading, a compulsive complimentary colouring that recalls Van Gogh's starry nights in which the stars blaze like biblical lamps in a blue midnight. It's thought they were given their name because although they look like particularly savage nettles, they don't sting. At this time of year, we gardeners are constantly finding self-seeded strangers, and most of them, like the yellow archangels, are wild flowers whose seeds and roots are still in the soil from before our housing estates and ribbon streets were built. Why not welcome them too? Why not allow our gardens to become holy ground? Even the most humble lawn dreams of its days as a wildwood glade.

The best gardeners are those who let the land be itself. Every garden, every park, every patch of wasteland, every motorway verge has its own memories and its reveries of the future.

After a gap of many years, swallows are nesting in our garage again. Eggs hidden high in their mud and straw nest in the rafters, their second brood hatched last week. Since then, the parents have been coming and going like flashes of blue lightning. Putting my sun lounger up in the front garden, I sat back to enjoy the swallow show. I wasn't disappointed. Time after time, they swooped over our car and darted into the garage: when feeding young, they'll dispose of about 6,000 flies a day; and with such carefree, dazzling panache. On a sleight of wing and tail fork, swallows can trick the human eye. Time after time I watched them leaving the garage, without having noticed them go in. Sometimes the pair met directly over me and air-danced, close enough for me to see their red throats. Plaintive, and ever louder as the afternoon progressed, the nestlings clamoured hungrily whenever a parent arrived: the toots of a toy squeeze-box. In our years without swallows, my heart weighed heavy each spring as I waited for them; this year, it flies as light and lissom as they do. To hear our swallows twittering and warbling as they rest momentarily on the telephone wire, tuning fork tails hanging down, is for me, the finest music on the planet.

*

What are your top ten soundtracks of nature?

It was the eels that made me late for the election count. Going into town to catch the bus, I stopped for a moment on the old Blakey bridge to peer down. The water, clear as the spring air, was inked with dark shapes: silhouetted crotchets and quavers hanging over the stave of the shallow stone bed. It's been a long time since I last saw an eel, and never like this, a score, two score of them idling on the flow. Still shrouded in mystery, our knowledge about eels is as faint as the moonless nights on which they begin their long migration, which takes them from places like our little beck, to the warm Sargasso Sea. Shadowy opposites of the celebrated salmon, the unsung eel lives a life in reverse to this other great fish traveller. Born in the warm Caribbean ocean, the tiny elver, see-through and utterly vulnerable, travels the ocean currents back to Europe where it heads inland up streams and even crosses fields, to find the perfect pool in which to grow to a slow maturity. When ready, taking fifteen years or so to grow to the typical metre, the eel will then swim back to its ancestral birth sea on the secret current-roads of the Atlantic Ocean. Only after 4,000 miles will they breed. Now, wasn't contemplating *that* journey worth missing a bus for?

Further encounters on this bridge showed me that these current-hangers were in fact lampreys, not eels. Nature offers us countless opportunities for being wrong. And then admitting it!

For five years I've watched this fish. Walking through the cornfields above our village to the beck at Thirkleby, I stand on the narrow footbridge and regularly view the brown trout's progress. When I first noticed a flicker in its little pool where the sunlight dapples the stone, the fish was no more than the size of my index finger; now it measures a foot, its length a brown ceramic decorated with dabs of red and black. The great Victorian naturalist Richard Jeffries also had a favourite trout that he watched under a bridge near London. Ever fearful that someone might bring a fishing rod, he was careful not to linger long enough to draw attention to its lie. I care for my trout too, but even in this day and age the bridge at Thirkleby is less frequented than Jefferies'. It's a so-called wake-way bridge, and was originally constructed for the funeral processions of villagers who died on the far side of the beck from where the church stands. These days its only traffic is the occasional dog walker, and the kingfisher who perches on the wooden rail. Running through a district of clay, for most of the year the beck is cloudy, the perfect cloak of invisibility for my friend the pool-dweller; only after periods of little or no rain does the water become as clear as it is today with the sun sparkling on the little pool and its wily but handsome lodger.

For me, this trout burns in its cold beck like a sanctuary lamp.

Hardly had the farmer finished ploughing the field last autumn, when the common field speedwell bloomed: blue eyes peeping out of the dark autumn mud. Flowering all the year round, these tiny gems are also called veronicas, being said to bear Christ's image like St Veronica's cloth. After the speedwell came the red dead-nettles and the yellow groundsel with its gift of seeds that feeds so many of our farmland birds. These wild flowers have been allowed to bloom in the special six metre border wrapped round the crop of wheat — an environmentally friendly practice attempting to minimise the damage of modern agriculture. Today, I noticed another flower in this road of colour. Wild pansies have no regulation colour. Sometimes yellow, other times violet; often petals of the same individual flower differ in hue. The flowers I could see were white with yellow stripes. Wild pansies have innumerable unofficial names. Heartsease refers to the sheer pleasure they give. The manner in which pansy stems ride up the long grass towards the light, gave rise to Johnny-jump-up. Such names as come-cuddle-me and jump-up-and-kiss-me testify to the flower's status as the special emblem of lovers. Not merely decorative, wild pansies provide a tea beneficial to various skin complaints. The land has a long memory, easily jogged by the judicious prod of a plough. It forgets nothing, waiting only for the opportunity to ease the heart.

Bees and butterflies are drawn to flowers. Why should we be any different?

Summer

The motorway meadows are coming into flower. My favourite one can be found on our local roundabout and up the slopes of the adjoining motorway embankment over which the traffic hurtles hysterically. The dandelions arrived first as though scattered in the night like fairy tale gold coins. Then the campion came, festooning the banks with red stars. The dog daisies soon followed, their brilliant flowers opening on unprepossessing stalks; and now the clover threads a thousand shades of red into the tapestry. The overall effect is staggering. Once mistaken for weeds, these plants combine to stitch together the elusive coat of splendour that no amount of Solomons or fashion gurus could ever hope to weave. Having largely disappeared from our landscape, our wild flower meadows thrive in places like waste ground, former industrial sites and along busy roads, which they accompany mile after mile like a continual offer of grace. Yesterday, the temptation proved too much. We stopped the car. Standing on the embankment, the meadow lapped at our knees like water. The sense of stillness was deepened by the crazed lumbering of the traffic all around. But though rooted in place, meadows are constantly in motion too: bees and butterflies journeying from flower to flower, the breeze constantly parting the knee-high sward, the ladybirds mounting stalks before flying off, and the dog daisies faithfully following the sun.

Beauty is found in the least expected places. And it asks us for nothing but admiration.

After the stile, the footpath had to muscle its way through a crowd of saplings. The leaves, shivering in the wind, were easy to identify. Only aspens quiver like this. No wonder they're also known as the shiver tree; it was as though a shudder was running through the little dell. The saplings' coppery green foliage wasn't the only thing shimmering; a nearby grove of mature aspens also waved in the wind. Even on still days aspens flutter; today, a blowy half-term afternoon, the trees clattered. Walking over a carpet of fluffy grey catkins cast by the mature trees, I approached the stand of large aspens. Light but durable, the wood of aspens like these would once have made oars, paddles, surgical splints. I say aspens, but there's a chance that this entire group of trees and saplings are actually a single organism. Despite the cast-off catkin seeds, often aspens spread by suckers, forming what are termed clonal colonies. In effect, all the aspens I was looking at might have been the same plant. Although each individual tree lives only into their forties, the roots of an aspen grove can be ancient. The oldest, in the mountains of Utah, is eighty thousand years old. Even this one might well be a thousand years. Or more. It's not every day you get to meet an arboreal Methuselah on an afternoon walk.

Living near trees is scientifically proven to make us feel younger!

If I were inventing a fairy tale, one of the characters would be a leaf-cutter bee. He'd be one of the good guys. All week I've been watching these perky insects visiting the borage under our window. Picture a slender version of the honey bee, and add a bright orange abdomen. In the shadows cast by our dense, blue flowers, the leaf cutters look like searching torch beams. Not only strikingly coloured, as they fly, their abdomens lift slightly as though offering a saddle to ride upon. In any fairy tale worth its salt, there would have to be an escape on the back of a friendly leaf cutter. Naturally, with the falling of night, the abdomen would light the way. Remarkably, the reality is hardly less amazing. Take their nest building. These bees select a leafy plant (in our garden, pumpkins are a popular choice) and then, with the skill of any fairy-tale tailor, expertly scissor away precise semi circles. These sections, often larger than the bee itself, are then flown to a hole in a tree or wall. Glued together with saliva, the pieces are crafted into a cigar shaped pod. Gummed up, the pod is then stocked with pollen and eggs. In here the bee's larvae can safely grow.

Both scientists and lovers of fairy tales can be astonished by the antics of the leaf-cutter bee.

Gardeners of the western world, why this relentless war against dandelions? Dandelions are one of nature's good guys. Growing in such profusion, they're a vital food source for wildlife; often the only food source. During our early, cold spring, I lost count of how many half-starved queen bees I found clinging to the yellow flowers like shipwrecked sailors to a life raft. Today, after a few dry weeks, our Goldfinches are feasting on the seeds. Their generosity extends as much to gardeners as it does to garden visitors. Far from ruining lawns or veg patches, dandelions offer a bespoke horticultural service. Not only are the golden flowers easy to grow and ravishingly beautiful, but their leaves are a ready-made peppery lettuce. Those deep tap roots, so often the demonised target of weed killer adverts, are also a gardener's friend; bringing up nutrients from the soil, they assist shallower rooted vegetables, and help keep the lawn green. Dandelions act as companion plants too. Research shows that by emitting ethylene gas, a ripening hormone, they help fruit to plump. But perhaps it's their loyalty that's the dandelion's most endearing characteristic. Originally a scarce plant of forest clearings and grasslands, it was human agriculture, with its continual disturbance of the soil that created the ideal dandelion environment. And they've been with us ever since. Enemies? No, companions. Faithful as dogs, they follow our heels.

Turn your garden into a peace zone — befriend dandelions.

This morning five tiny beaks are peeping over the rim of the mud cup high up in the garage rafters. As we peer up at them, a great chirping breaks out. Even though their parents feed them from dawn to dusk — 18 hours in these northerly midsummer days — the Swallow nestlings are always hungry. We can hear them from every room in our house: the ravenous greetings of the young, and the tender babbling of their adults. The bedroom window upstairs gives us the best view of their aerodynamics. A sheen of countless blues glistens from their backs as they bullet into the garage; a deft tilt of wing and forked tail dipping them under the raised door at the very last moment. Seconds later, the parent Swallow darts free like a fish. Red throats flashing, they lift and swoop steeply, playing in the shallows of the air over our little garden. Unlike most animals, Swallows actively seek out human habitation. For many thousands of years we have lived together. Even before language developed, humans were enjoying their songs and flight displays. European culture considers it good luck to have them as lodgers. Last year's broods got to know our family so well that when they returned this spring, they danced all around us, swooping within joyous inches of our heads, calling ecstatically. We were a recognised part of their environment; the landbound, slow-moving objects around which they could plot their flights of fancy.

When I die, I pray that Swallows will be waiting, perched on the pearly gates, twittering their ancient welcome. And if there's silence? I'll know I've come to the wrong place.

The clouds were low. Water dripped from every bent grass head. Each flower was bowed with raindrops. So when I reached the fallow land by the woods, I was amazed to find the thick, sodden vegetation shimmering with butterflies. I knew bumble bees fly in quite heavy rain, but here were butterflies doing the same. The dusky, almost black butterflies were Ringlets. As the Ringlets flickered about the soaked grasses, their dark velvety wings framed with a white border, caught what little light there was. Passing me, they seemed to flash. Ringlets don't need direct sun; their sombre colouring allows them to warm up more quickly than brighter coloured insects. The same is true of another species darting around me in the rain, the slightly lighter coloured, Meadow Brown. Their habit of flying on dreich, cheerless days has earned both butterflies a strange reputation for sorrow. *Maniola,* the Latin name for Meadow Browns, refers to the spirits of the dead; whilst the French call Ringlets, Le Tristan. This odd connotation continued with the third species of damp day flier that I found feeding on a thistle. The black and white Marbled White was once called Our Half Mourner. But there could be nothing funereal about my next butterfly encounter. Huge eyed and fox cub orange, the Common Skipper shone like a piece of costume jewellery worn at a party.

Watching butterflies is like learning a new language.

I've been here before often, yet on each visit I can never quite believe it's real. First of all, you turn off the main road. Main road? Not exactly a motorway – the long-horned cattle in the field have far more hikers to gaze at than cars. A gate lures you onto a road even less well trodden. To the left a steep bank of oaks rises to the place where we once saw a herd of red deer. To the right, through willows, you glimpse flashes of ultramarine blue on the narrow valley bottom. These are the fish ponds built by the monks at Rievaulx. The ponds are a clue but nothing can fully prepare you for what is waiting when the trees suddenly thin. Reaching a little summit, the path hurries you down through a meadow to where broad stepping stones offer a beck of sheet glass clarity. You have reached the springs at the head of Nettle Dale. One of the smallest and lesser known corners of our Hambleton Hills, but for me, a Shangri-La. It was a hot day and we went straight to the water. Gurgling over a gravel bed, here the stream is only yards from its source where it bubbles up in the bank. Gasping at the coldness, we drank great handfuls, the cascading drops counted by the sun.

We all have our 'promised land', our special places of laughter, love and hope.

Standing on the bridge at Thirsk station, you can see for miles. The countryside stretches away like a deep, green lake. I was admiring the distant island of an oak wood when I noticed a figure on the tracks below. It was a tatty tabby cat. He'd chosen a bad place for a stroll; at that moment a whistle announced the imminent thunder-through of the Edinburgh Express. Passengers were advised to step back from the platform edge. As the train approached, a Blackbird in the siding stopped singing. Rabbits scattered. But the cat continued to amble along. Only when he felt the vibrations of the track did he at last take evasive action. A first leap onto the platform failed. Likewise a second. At the third attempt, the tabby gained a claw hold. Just in time. The express shot by, sending a shiver through the red valerian flowers growing from the walls of the waiting room. The Blackbird resumed its song. The rabbits re-emerged. It was then I saw that the cat was three legged. 'Oh aye,' said the ticket office man, stroking him. 'Folk are always worrying he's been killed.' Rolling over, the three-legged cat purred. A butterfly fluttered past. On the siding, bees floated in the low clover, the dog roses continued to bloom. From the adjoining allotment, a cockerel crowed. The cat lay back in the sun.

Modest places always have the most to offer.

Over the years I've found myself dealing with many kinds of nocturnal visitors. Rats in the rafters, bats in the bedroom, ram raiders at the door and, when we lived in South Africa, honey badgers wolfing down birthday cake in the kitchen. Last night's commotion began just before midnight — a cacophony of snorting and snuffling, huffing and puffing, wheezing and whining. I could hardly believe it. Wild boar in deepest Yorkshire? I crept out the back door. Although silent now, the noise had come from round the side of the house. I approached cautiously, only to find not hogs but hedgehogs. Two of them were facing each other in what looked like a standoff. Suddenly, a bout of head-butting and chasing. Trying not to laugh out loud at my misidentification and disturb the show, I watched the victor return alone. A smaller hedgehog suddenly slipped out from behind a plant pot. What I had just seen was the male driving off a rival; now the breeding could begin. The 'hedgehog rutting season' is in full swing. As the male and female circled each other, the snorting and snuffling began again. It went on for hours. Shakespeare too must have been kept awake by the leisurely courtship of hedgehogs, because when his witches prepared their brew, they had to wait until: 'Thrice and once the hedgepig whined.' That's a lot of whining!

Is your garden hedgehog friendly?

Sometimes being lost is the best place to be. Where was I? Emerging from woods, the horizon offered a field of cattle and a winding road. I accepted. A pair of bubbling becks kept me company, and three cattle grids later, I reached a farm. No one about. A Blackcap singing in a willow drew me to a gate. I climbed it. And that's how I found the moat. The willow grew on the side of a deep gully. No naturally occurring ghyll this, I followed it a little way and saw that the ravine curved itself artfully round a raised mound. I reached for my map. Miles from where I thought I was, a moat was marked. The farm beside the moat was Tang Hall Farm (Tang being Anglo Saxon for where two becks meet: think tongs). Had the farm got its name from an old hall that once stood on the mound? It must have been an important place to be protected by such an impressive fortification. Dried up now, sides overgrown and boggy bottom lost in yellow flag iris, the moat was thirty feet deep and just as wide. Crossing the moat on a land bridge, watched by a herd of freshly sheared Swaledale sheep I ascended the mound. A few stones studded the pasture – crumbs from an old manor house? Ozymandias in the green fields of England.

*

To find yourself, you first have to be lost.

Is there ever a truly still day? Open the window even on summer afternoons and you'll find yourself inviting in a breeze that will shuffle your papers and belly your blinds. Sleep with unlatched windows and you'll hear that same playful hand twitching the curtains. A strong wind is the washing line's friend, but can soon grow tetchy, slamming doors and windows. Powerful winds are bracing, especially sea breezes, and autumn gales are exhilarating as they sing through the trees. It's even fun to spend an hour or so bent into a vertical blizzard pretending to be Captain Scott slugging it to the Antarctic. Whatever the season, there's a blow to go with it. We'd be lonely without our restless friend. Then came the hottest day of the year. Not a breath stirred. A relentless sun brought out the butterflies, browned the barley, and turned homes and offices into saunas. Panting in the heat I lay in the deepest shade, but couldn't get comfortable. The Sparrows bathed in the pond. Both hens and grass cried out for water. Then I felt something cool and tender touch my cheek. The faithful breeze hadn't forgotten us. Gently it eased its fingers through what's left of my hair.

Watching and listening, lying around on a summer's day, is never a waste of time.

There's an old saying: whoever wishes to see the world should stay in the same place. I thought of this today strolling along one of my favourite walks. I come this way at least twice a week, and although every step is entirely familiar, from this path I have indeed encountered travellers from every corner of the world. Just there where the barley is now browning, I once saw a flock of Snow Buntings from Finland; in the branches of the oak under which the bridleway passes, the first Cuckoo of the year used to sit having just arrived from Africa. Halfway to the woods I have previously encountered a Little Stint fresh from the Arctic, and in the woods themselves grow thickets of rhododendrons, which were brought from Japan by the local landowner a century since. In the woods too of course, there's the grey squirrel from across the Atlantic. *Whoever wishes to see the world should stay in the same place.* But it's not just visitors from distant places that one encounters on this path. Amongst the beans a colony of white flowers is blooming. This plant grows here every year whatever the crop, the soil still holding it in its seed bank from the Middle Ages when the flower was grown here on a large scale due to its properties as a cleaning agent. The flower is called soapwort. Each footpath, however humble, takes you to the rest of the world, and into history itself.

The most radical pilgrimage of all is the epic odyssey of discovering the ground beneath your feet.

The rain caught me on the lane. Dashing for the grey-walled church, I sheltered in the porch. Water cascaded from the guttering as I peered out at the churchyard. One section had been left unmown for wildlife, and there, the scatter of old, forgotten gravestones seemed to wade waist deep through the midsummer grass. In the wash of the custard-coloured meadowsweet, rosebay willowherb and the lapis lazuli blue of meadow crane's bill, something rarer grew. Well over a metre tall, each thick stem bearing countless nodding, glossy, dark maroon flowers, the Martagon lilies lifted themselves up above the crowd. Though still raining, I had to take a closer look. The long-stalked anthers were fiery ginger; when I touched one, a heady perfume wafted out. What were they doing here? Non-natives, brought to Britain as garden plants, Martagon lilies were first recorded growing wild in 1782. Still rare today, had they spread here from a local garden, or were they a memento of old burials? In Victorian times, Martagon lilies were a popular funeral flower; perhaps a bunch was laid on one of these graves, died, seeded and slowly grew into this colony. The names on the gravestones might be forgotten, but the Martagon lilies still bloom, a reminder that nature's memory lasts a lot longer than ours.

*

Why are our places of death also our places of life?

There's nothing for raising the spirits like seeing the first thistle in bloom. No wonder Crabbie's decorate their bottles of alcoholic ginger beer with them. As swallows arriving in April are a sign that the world still works, so the pale purple July flowers open like a fulfilled promise. In our ever-shrinking natural world, blighted by pesticide poison, factory farming and lawn mowers, thistles are a rallying call for free-range habitats, a memory of life before fences. They are a sign that the land around them is *not* an 'intensive-agriculture desert' but full of life. You can't blame them for having spikes, how else can they jostle for elbow room in a crowded planet? Steeples of biodiversity, even in the rain, they're a magnet to insects. Their variety is stunning, from the graceful nodding thistle, which is half sunflower and half cactus, to the melancholy thistle, named not because of its appearance, which is jaunty to the point of perkiness, but because people used to eat it as a cure for melancholia. Without spikes, the melancholy thistle was said by herbalists to make you cheery as a cricket. Not all thistles have the lovely magenta colour. The carline thistle has the golden brown bear cub fur, and the sow thistle is lemon.

If the earth could pray, it would have a litany of thistles.

The heat wasn't making things any better. In the sweltering city centre café I stared blankly at the laptop screen. Was it two or three weeks' worth of work I'd just lost, or months' worth? I stumbled outside. Eyes screwed up against the sunlight dazzling off steel and glass, I wandered despondently through Leeds' central business district. Coming to a bench shaded by a tall tree, I sat down. The lime tree rose high above me, a living column whose light green canopy formed a thick, sheltering parasol. The air underneath was cool, fresh; it felt as though I was sitting neck deep in welcome cold water. Slowly, my breathing eased. Were things really so bad? Well, yes, but then — couldn't I hear bees? I peered up. Miles from any garden or meadow, the bees had also found the tree, and were gathering honeydew from the leaves, and nectar from the flowers. Their hum soothed the city din, turning this corner of Leeds into a woodland glade. Lime flower tea is famous for its tranquil properties, and I felt the tree calming me. After all, even if I wrote for another hundred years could I say anything better than this: one hot day in the city, caught in the woes of the moment, I sheltered for a while beneath a lime tree, and listened to the bees?

Go and choose your favourite city tree, and spend some time with it.

There are still so many surprises left. Like the scent of a bean field wafting up the lane to meet you. Or the fact that a comfrey flower takes forty minutes to fill back up with nectar once a bee has emptied it, whilst bird's foot trefoil takes a whole day and a night. And then there's *vespa crabro*, the European hornet. Having lived my life in the north of England, I'd never encountered one before, but recently they've been spreading up from the south east. Nothing could have prepared me for the shock of seeing one suddenly flying out of the bird box. Two-and-a-half inches long, hooped with yellow and terracotta red, the queen hornet bore down on me. As though freshly escaped from a fairy tale, it buzzed in my face and stared eye to eye, demanding my credentials. European hornets, our largest social wasp species, are so big that at first you can't believe they're real. Yet despite their size, experts stress that they're pretty laid back; they even call them gentle giants. That night, still moved by the hornet's size and grace, I went out on my usual veg patch slug patrol. A buzzing sound was followed by wings fanning my face. Hornets have such powerful eyes that they can fly on moonlit nights.

There is always something new to discover.

Our path took us through the ripening barley. Above us, the sky was blue and vast as a sea. The morning hush seemed to hold everything in its arms: the great oaks, the scarlet poppies, the Yellowhammer drowsing on the hedge. We were artists searching for a subject and the little bridge we came to, arcing over the stream, seemed ideal. My son and I clambered over the fence, and wound our way down through the meadow to the beckside where two lush cushions of grass awaited us like thrones. Having made our sketches, we began to add colour, using water scooped from the rivulet itself. But how to capture the sunlight dappling the old stone, and the way the white wooden railings were worn by generations of passing hands, and the grooves made by the elbows of those stopping to gaze? And how to render the tinkle of the stream itself as it played over its gravel and stones, and the wind gently ruffling the hair of the willow growing aslant the brook? Then of course, there was the fresh smell of sweet water and rich growth; could that be captured on paper? As we worked, a pair of horses watched us from the other side. In the distance a family was haymaking their single acre. *That's good*, my son said, whose age is about that of my artistic ability, *I like the way you've made the water seem to flow from the sky.*

This is one of the sacred moments of my life. Part of me will always be painting by that beck.

The story is as old as humanity. In the red corner we have the industrious, though dour ant who works all year preparing for winter; in the blue, the fiddle playing, goodtime grasshopper, who spends summer making music, and then the first cold breath of winter blows and .... Whoever first told that story was neither a musician, nor understood grasshoppers! This afternoon, winter still mercifully distant, I lay with the grasshoppers on the steep bank above the chapel at Scotch Corner. The rest of the world was dog days silent, but the long grass all around me was filled with the famous chirping. These are the males calling to the females. Their serenading, made by a row of pegs on the back legs playing against forewings, is known as stridulation. Experts can identify our thirty species of UK grasshopper by their different sound. We're in a heat wave and as the temperature rose, everything seemed to doze. Even the ubiquitous, little brown butterflies lost their briskness. The breeze itself closed its eyes. The grasshoppers alone grafted. Showing no signs of hanging up their fiddles, on and on they played as though for some Aesopian ceilidh. Occasionally, like a dancer moved by music, one would vault me. If we could jump as high, we'd be leaping over our own homes.

Are you a grasshopper or an ant?

I was wheeling out the bins under a bright blue sky when I saw the Banded Demoiselle. What else could it be, that large damselfly perching on the branch? I'd seen them in books and documentaries before, on YouTube too, but I'd never believed I could encounter something so astounding on my own front drive. We often enjoy the more common blue tailed damselfly at the garden pond, and various dragonfly species, but this was like a visitor from another world. Not only is the Banded Demoiselle our largest damselfly, it's our most characterful. A large pair of goggle eyes stared at me; its body was a whole blue-green peacock crammed into an inch and a half of damselfly; and a fingerprint was banded across each folded wing — that's where their name comes from. I called my son and we stared in admiration. But if the Banded Demoiselle was arresting enough in repose, when it lifted from the branch, it became utterly magical. Whirling and dancing around us, it glinted in an ethereal shimmer. More butterfly than damselfly, the blue-green peacock sheen of its body was lit by a white 'tail light' on the underside of its latter abdominal segments; its four, blue-black thumb-printed wings, broad and nearly as long as its body, seemed to glitter like a midnight disco ball.

Even something as mundane as putting the bins out can be an invitation to change your life.

China has its pandas, India its tigers, and the River Ouse its tansy beetles. The size of an abacus bead, shining green body imprinted with a rainbow, the tansy beetle is just as endangered as those better-known species. Equally wild, and in its own way equally beautiful, this little insect is equally worth saving. Once widespread across the UK, they're now limited to a thirty-mile stretch of Yorkshire's River Ouse. One of the most accessible places to experience these treasures is the former abbey of St Mary's in York Museum Gardens. Here the Tansy Beetle Champions Project has planted plots of the beetle's exclusive food source – the tansy plant. Take a walk down to the fourteenth-century Hospitium and you'll find these rarities shining like gems amongst the yellow button flowers of the raggedy tansy. If the sun comes out you'll see why they've become known as the Jewel of York. Other conservation measures include fencing off 'tansy islands' along the river. Rarely flying, and unable to detect their food plant by scent – pungent though it be to us – these 'tansy islands' must be close enough together for the beetle to stumble upon when walking. Yes, the world needs its bamboo forests and savannahs, but it also needs ungrazed, unfertilised, rampantly ragged riverbanks where the tansy plant, and its living, enigmatic jewel, nods sleepily over slow waters.

There is a priceless preciousness in the roughest, raw, most 'unspectacular' places.

At this time of year, the verges and unmown pastures are beginning to look gloriously shaggy. Many plants have already flowered and seeded. The froth of Queen Anne's lace is just a memory; the hogweed is a leaning tower of brown. All the delicacy of spring and early summer might have passed, but there's one plant whose beauty is still at its height. Unobtrusive, in fact often hidden from the human eye, *stachys sylvatica,* or woundwort, is currently lighting up the shadows in a hedgerow near you. Thriving in even the shadiest corner, just to look at woundwort's tall, soda fountain froth of purple flowers etched with a fizz of white scribbles, is to slake your thirst. But although its flowers rival the orchid, its pungent scent is foul — at least to us humans. Try rubbing its nettle-like leaves and you'll see what I mean. Yet many insects find it irresistible. Bumble bees hunt it out, and the wool carder solitary bee likes woundwort so much that it builds its territory round it. Our largest solitary bee, the chunky wool carder is a bit of a trickster. Coloured more like a wasp than a bee to deter predators, it has the perky flight character of a hover fly. Then there's the woundwort shield bug. This tiny insect, glinting in the sun like a bronze coin, won't willingly feed on any other plant.

Nature, the great babushka doll. Nothing stands alone, we're all wrapped inside something else, inside something else, inside something else ....

I'm sitting in the old coastguard tower on the sea cliffs rising above Northumbria's Holy Island of Lindisfarne. From here you can see the whole island and its vast setting of sea and sky. Last night, gales yelled over the huddle of red roofed houses and weathered priory stones; today the wind has dropped, and the North Sea wears an almost tranquil smile. The boats barely bob in the tear-shaped little harbour. Only the waves breaking on the far headland show a snarl of white. The tide is coming in and the weathered pilgrim stilts marking the causeway are slowly drowning. The sandbanks, black with basking seals, steadily shrink. Soon the seals will head out to hunt for cod or haddock, but for a while longer they lie there singing on their dwindling island. It's worth coming here just to witness the seal song, an eerie, plaintive, other-wordly chorus that matches the howling of wolves and the din of snorting buffalo for sheer wildness. The seals breed seven kilometres out to sea on the Farne Islands that ride the horizon like sperm whales. They then return to Lindisfarne and the rest of the North East coast. Most of them are grey seals. Britain has eighty per cent of the European population of this species. As I'm gazing at the seals, a gull flies by the tower, meets my eye, holds it.

'Be not afeared. The air is full of noises, sounds and sweet airs that give delight and hurt not.' (William Shakespeare)

A great year for peacock butterflies. Everywhere you go these colourful harlequins tumble at you from above, before rearing off again. Flying on surprisingly vigorous wings they dart through the shallows of the sky like tropical fish over the reef of back gardens. One settled on my leg as I sat reading, its long tongue testing the fabric of my blue shorts for nectar. Only when the page turned did it fly off. As summer wanes, butterflies are our consolation prize. These glad-ragged insects delight, from their roar of colour on our neighbours' buddleia with its record of twenty-five butterflies, to the solitary common blue, who, though tiny, seems a scrap of the vast harvest sky. This August, a speckled wood butterfly has taken up residence in our back garden. Brown wings splashed with yellow, its colouring perfectly mirrors the woodland glade's dappled shade of its natural home. Trying to work this morning, the speckled wood drew me repeatedly from my desk. A drama was unfolding. A single, ripe apple hung from a bough, and the butterfly was feeding on it with gusto. Others wanted the treat too however, and every time a wasp appeared, the speckled wood fluttered away. A sting would be fatal. All morning, a procession of wasps glutted themselves on the fermenting fruit; the speckled wood, watching and waiting, darted in when the opportunity arose, before weaving away just in time.

What are your *consolations of the waning summer?*

We stepped off the train into the fine, soft Manchester rain. We were still inside Piccadilly Station but the drops were seeping through the roof. It felt like the perfect reception – my son and I were in town to see the singer Morrissey, Poet Laureate of northern melancholia. By the time we got outside, clouds had lifted and the sunlight catching the raindrops on a tram, turned it into a gem encrusted chariot. I've lived so long on the other side of the Pennines that I've almost forgotten the tender touch of west coast rain. Later, at a pavement café, drinking tea with a taste of the Lake District (where Manchester gets its water), I welcomed another shower. Staring up at the slate grey sky, at first I thought that the large bird flying overhead was a Great Black-backed Gull. It wasn't until it had passed the cathedral spire that I wondered if it was a migrating Osprey. One of the birds from Loch Garten perhaps, or Bassenthwaite, on its way to Africa? Strip away the urban sprawl and Greater Manchester is ideal Osprey territory. Salford is thirty per cent peat bog. Imagine the number of Ospreys that used to fish there before the cotton mills and the smoke. Is it too much to hope that these graceful riverine raptors will one day grace Manchester again?

*

Summer comes, summer dies. Yesterday my son was a toddler, today he is a young man. The sweet, sad joys of mortality.

Autumn

The days shorten; the mornings grow chilly. Autumn is arriving. But though the grass is dying, the wild flowers fading and the leaves will soon be falling, not all colour is draining from the world. In fact, September always saves some of the year's most scintillatingly vivid sights for itself. I was sitting reading by the garden pond on a sunny afternoon, when I heard a clattering in the logs that frame the little pool. Nothing could prepare me for what I saw a moment later. Southern hawker dragonflies are large; by Northern European standards they're massive. The individual I could see hovering over the dead wood was nearly three inches long, with a wingspan not much shorter. But it wasn't just the size. The dragonfly was a glazed brilliance of greens and yellows; it was as though an ancient Roman mosaic had come to life. Neither was she in any hurry. All afternoon, no more than two yards from me, she continued laying eggs in the logs. Southern hawkers lay hundreds in their lives, especially on calm, sunny September days. Miracles take time. These eggs won't hatch until spring, and then the nymph larvae will crawl into the pond, where they'll hide in the murk of weed and rotting leaves, before emerging into the sunshine of a distant September, three years from now.

I'd never won the lottery, until the day the hawker dragonfly arrived.

I was sitting at the open window reading when I heard a strange chirping sound in the garden. I went to investigate. After a disappointing August, it was a pleasantly warm night outside. Walking to the back wall, I realised that the sound was coming from somewhere in our neighbour's scrub. And that it could only be a cricket. I've heard them in Africa and in Italy but never in Britain. Was it possible? That constant, undeviating purring of the night seemed so uncharacteristic of North Yorkshire that I wondered whether it was a new climate change phenomenon. On and on it went. Zoologists once measured this creature's output and reckoned that a single cricket had called 42,000 times during one nightshift. Folklore often characterised the cricket as a fiddler, not a bad guess since the song is created by the bowing of its wing-casing against hind legs. In ancient China the sound was so valued as a sleeping aid that people kept the insects in bedside cages; European affection for them is measured in its literature. In both Charles Dickens' *The Cricket on the Hearth* and Collodi's *Pinocchio*, the singing cricket is a voice of benevolent wisdom; although a warning note is sounded in the cautionary tale of the ant and the grasshopper — a stand in for the cricket — in which the insect is punished for fiddling away the summer months instead of labouring. Back at the window I listened as the night deepened.

This just happened once in the seventeen years we've lived here. Nox Mirabilis!

I'm so glad I was late sowing my runner beans this year. Now that most of our other garden flowers have bloomed and faded, the runner beans are still going strong. Scented towers of brilliant scarlet, they're just what the bumble bees are looking for. We always eat runner beans young, when the soft green pods resemble the curled boots in the story of *The Elves and the Shoemaker*. A few pods are left to grow to their maximum, and we use these beans to sow next year. It's these seed runner beans that cast us right into the middle of another fairy tale. Who hasn't heard of *Jack and the Beanstalk*? Well, if you've ever felt a handful of the glinting tortoiseshell beans for yourself then you'll understand why he swapped the family cow for them. Easy too to see the inspiration behind the idea of the magic beanstalk becoming a stairway to the great riches of a giant's castle. Even though it's September now, the bean plants are still growing apace. In a transaction not without its own magic, I was given my first beans by an old allotmenteer in Gateshead, who said that they were 'descended' from some his grandfather had given him between the wars. And he didn't even ask me for anything in return.

Tardiness can be a much-maligned pastime.

At the moment life feels like one long goodbye. Swallows are departing, House Martins gathering and bumble bees slipping away into hibernation. Last weekend, on perhaps the final warm Saturday of the year, I sat working with the windows open; one after the other some of my summer companions drifted in as though bidding farewell. First of all, loud buzzing announced a wasp. Droning heavily around the room, for a few moments it landed on my keyboard before heading back out the way it came. Next, a red admiral butterfly gained entry and filled the room with colour and life. Chances are this is the offspring of migrants — most UK red admirals arrive here from central Europe in spring and early summer, they then lay eggs, which mature into adults about now. As the butterfly careered around, its deceptively powerful wings fanned my face. I guided it to the window. Liberated, it flew out into Yorkshire like a scrap of magic carpet. Later that evening I was reading, when a daddy-long-legs blundered inside and fumbled about the room like a tiny hobby horse. It might lack a wasp's power, and the graceful strength of a continent-bestriding butterfly, but it too deserved to enjoy its day of life in the open air. The first frost will kill it. *Adios,* I whispered, setting the insect free, *until we meet again ....*

Eventually we all have to say goodbye to those we love. We can only choose how to do so.

We've been preparing the garden for its winter sleep. The carrots are still growing but the cabbage is finished so we turned the soil over and dug in the contents of our compost heap, a mixture of nutrients that has been brewing nicely all summer. The frosts will do the rest. Having collected the last seeds from the micro meadow, we gathered the twigs and hedge clippings to use as insulation for our conversion of the log pile into the Hedgehog Hotel. It was as we were clearing out the nest boxes that the summer divulged one of its closest kept secrets. From March to August, our sparrow terrace had been in constant use. A pair of tree sparrows had used each of the three separate chambers in turn; no sooner fledging one brood before building a home for the next. Opening the box and bringing out three surprisingly substantial nests, not only could we see that each brood had been successful but we could name the materials out of which their parents had so lovingly constructed their homes. Along with the moss, twigs, catkins, grass and feathers, we found six inches of blue twine, the orange tag from a black bin liner, and a child's finger length of bright red wool from the jumper our little boy wore when he was learning to walk. The September breeze tugged at the red thread that had nurtured young life twice.

Life hangs by these threads.

I can never pass a field maple without stopping. Smaller, native cousin of the showy sycamore, this gem of a tree leads an unassuming life hidden in the hedges and wood edges. 'Easily overlooked,' one guide says. 'Unobtrusive,' states another. For a long time, I thought the tiny-leafed field maple was merely a kindly hawthorn, a friendly variant growing without the thorns. But if our only native maple is self-effacing in its natural habitat, when it meets the human hand things change. As well as being the main choice for carving and turning, for centuries this slow grown, tough wood has been the home of our most beautiful music. Antonio Stradivari favoured it above all other trees for his celebrated violins, and even further back, harps were framed with maple, one being found preserved in the burial chamber at Sutton Hoo. After a life resounding with the Blackcap and Nightingales, an afterlife of human melody. The field maple also harbours a fascinating legend within its dense, dark green canopy. A recalcitrant fieldworker was once hung on one for protesting against a landowner's enclosing of publicly owned space. Refusing to oppress its fellow hedge dweller, the tree snapped in two, and to this day remains small, so that it can't be used as a gallows of oppression. I can never pass a field maple without stopping.

Sometimes fact and fiction blur into a pleasant, dappled light, like the autumn sun through the tired canopy of a field maple.

The generous early autumn sun sank but the warmth lingered in the garden, so I did too. Who knows, I thought, maybe it will be the last mild evening of the year. Slowly, night pooled out from under the apple tree and began to lap around my feet. In their nest under the eaves, the House Martin family whirred and ticked like a clock. And then the bats came out. We haven't seen them all year and my heart rose at the sight of the serrated silhouettes flickering above me. The darting, erratic flight patterns identified them as common pipistrelles. Wings crackling on the growing darkness, they played round and round our 1970s semi like shadow House Martins. And like House Martins, they hoovered up the insects. Common pipistrelles can eat 3,000 insects in a night. By now the female bats will have left June's maternity roosts and will be ready to breed again. The bats I could see were the males searching for a mate. What I couldn't hear was the love songs they were singing – their calls are above normal adult hearing frequency. In the middle distance, Tawny Owls called; in the sky, the stars were coming out. Swooping at a moth, one bat came almost within reach, then whisked back round the house with mesmeric agility. With each passing flight, the dark deepened until at last I could see nothing but the stars.

Time to befriend your shadow?

It's never easy saying goodbye, especially on mornings like this. As I hang the washing out, the air has that freshness unique to autumn mornings; it's as though I'm the first person ever to breathe it — the first person ever to breathe. The sky is deepest blue. The all-seeing light picks out all the details of the morning's masterpiece: the red haw berries, the gnats drifting companionably about my head and the House Martins gathering above. One by one the summer visitors have all left: the Swifts, the Swallows, the Blackcaps. Now the House Martins' time has come. Nesting in the eaves of our little house, they've filled our days with grace, weaving their lives into ours. Every time we come and go, they are there. As we work, as we talk — there they are too, working, talking. We worried about them when they struggled to find mud for their nests in the hot, dry summer; and we've been moved when the parents lead their children out of the nests for the first time and into the vast world. Now, I'm pausing to watch them for perhaps the last time this year. If I was ever to construct a mythology, I would have the world created on an autumnal morning like this.

Life is that wild, wonderful gift between hello and goodbye.

We were rounding up the hens for our next-door neighbour when we saw the shape perched on the telegraph wire. Utterly motionless and head down as it scanned the rough grass below, this wasn't something we'd ever seen round here before. Breath ragged with excitement, we stalked through the trees for a closer look and had almost got the bird in range when it flew off. Was it a Kestrel? Similar, but too fast, this raptor was shooting over the cricket pitch on stiff, turbo charged wings. A Peregrine? Too small. The diminutive falcon landed on the dilapidated pavilion roof from where it continued to hunt. This time we got close enough to see the tip of its tail: dark as bilberries. It could only be a Merlin. The smallest UK bird of prey, Merlins breed on the upland moors and then in autumn they come to their lowland farmland hunting grounds. In these weeks of the great migration, as millions of birds sift silently through our lives southbound for different continents, some, like our Merlin, may only travel a few miles for their winter quarters, nevertheless they bring a breath of the exotic. I've been walking these fields for years and have never seen anything like the Merlin. When it lit up again and darted low over the stubble, the falcon reached the distant woods in seconds.

How I love these little local backwaters of the great rivers of migration.

Was this the last warm day of the year? The stubble fields below glinted in the afternoon sun, the hawthorns climbing the rise seemed to have fallen asleep. Wheeling through the little lanes and winding roads of the Hambleton Hills, I pulled in at my favourite stretch of beck and had lunch under the packhorse bridge. Feet dangling in the stream, reflected sunlight dancing on the arch above me, I listened to the play of water echoing against the stonework. Downstream, beyond the crowfoot beds, lay the remnants of the wheel-house from the days when a watermill ground corn here. When I got up for a closer look, a shadow darted down the beck. It was a bullhead fish. Bullheads, odd looking animals with bulging eyes on a large, flattened head, huge fan-like fins and a tapering body, are also known as the 'miller's thumb'. Living in the kind of remote, fast flowing streams favoured by watermills, perhaps the fish's head was reminiscent of a miller's digit which became flattened by years of sifting flour between thumb and forefinger to gauge texture. Or was it a sly reference to a miller's reputation of pressing on the scales with a thumb to cheat customers of a few pounds of flour?

When was the last time a history lesson was this much fun?

There were four of them wrapped snugly in the dead seed head. I paused in my task of digging up the clump of last year's musk mallows, and looked closer. Many of the other seed heads I was about to pull up were also filled with ladybird lodgers hoping to overwinter in these desirable digs. Ladybirds are hard to resist. In most cultures they have won a special place in people's hearts. Their name often expresses our affection for them; in Gaelic they are known as *bhóin Dé,* meaning God's Little Cow, whilst in Yiddish they are known as Moses' little cow. In Britain, the term *Lady Bird* dedicates this useful little beetle to Jesus' mother, a link made in the Middle Ages when the Virgin was depicted in scarlet. In Argentina they belong to St Anthony. More recently, ladybirds were nominated as the emblem insect for no fewer than six American states. In Indonesia too, they are often seen as a symbol of good luck. Perhaps it's their sudden, pleasing flight that has made them the subject of rhymes in many different nations. Usually of the fly-away variety, in Portugal these rhymes have the insects flying to Lisbon, whilst in Turkey they are encouraged to go and collect slippers and shoes. Knowing all of this how could I evict such welcome tenants? I lifted up my garden fork and passed over the hibernation corner untouched.

It's hard to be lonely in a world with ladybirds.

It wasn't exactly the most promising of places or times for a moth encounter. Mid-morning, and I was sitting sipping a caffè latte on Teesside University's new plaza. Although it was October, the sun glinted on the metal street furniture. The passing students seemed excited with the newness of their learning. I was reading a poem about moths when — along came a moth. A purposeful whirring flight brought the humming bird hawk moth right to my table. It hovered over my coffee for a moment before darting away into the depths of the campus. I got up and followed. It flew faster than I could run but it wasn't going far. I caught up with the striking insect as it hovered over a raised flowerbed, one of the university's beautiful new 'green spaces'. Long proboscis sipping nectar, gingery wings aflame, harlequin abdomen a chequered flag, and large eyes strangely earnest, the moth went from flower to flower. A passing student, similarly fascinated, got out a phone and recorded the sighting for *The Butterfly Conservation's* Migrant Watch. Every year hummingbird hawk moths visit us from North Africa. Our Swallows and House Martins might have gone, but these enigmatic, day flying visitors keep the summer alive. The row of raised flowerbeds, placed between the Human Resources department and the multi-storey 'DigitalCity' Athena building, was literally a lifeline.

Autumn can also be the time to say hello.

Something beautiful is blooming between Middlesbrough and Thornaby. Among the scented minarets of the buddleias, birch trees and the bramble thickets that thrive on the disused railway sidings and platforms, a colony of blue-purple flowers is coming into brilliant, autumn flower. Having escaped from nearby back gardens, the perennial aster is currently offering travellers the exotic gift of a deep blue October. Free from herbicides, railway land has long since become a precious environment, opening its arms to species no longer allowed to flourish elsewhere. Toads and frogs find a home here too. Foxes and voles. Apple trees also grow on railway land, planted by decades of passengers scrunching their fruit and then throwing the core through the window. Some apple varieties thought to be lost, have been rediscovered in embankment orchards. Orchids too. Last night, pulling slowly out of Thornaby I noticed evening primroses growing among the blue Teesside train track asters: suns in a cloudless sky. As I was enjoying their scent through the open window, there was a slap on the page of my notebook. A hawthorn shield bug had flown in. Green and brown, the bug was shaped like a shield. As I guided it back out, a pheasant called from under a rusting diesel chassis. Like the asters and the evening primroses, pheasants are not native, having been brought here by the Romans. Well, it looked perfectly at home here in the track bed and siding wilderness.

*

The scorched places of the earth have the gentlest of rebirths.

The plan seemed fool proof: one of us climb up and give the tree an almighty shake whilst the rest stand underneath with a sheet to catch the loosened fruit. This year however the boughs are so heavily laden that a single shake brought down a hail of apples, pelting heads and drumming shoulders. Easier just to pick through the windfalls, and keep the unbruised ones for storing. It's national apple week, and time to harvest the orchard fruits. Is there a greater work of art than an apple freshly picked, especially if a single green leaf is still attached? The fragrance, the promise of flavour, the way it sits in the palm of your hand. Impossible not to take a bite. No wonder mythology often thrusts apples into the limelight. Adam and Eve receive the doubtful gift of knowledge by eating one, not in the 'official' bible of course where the forbidden fruit is nonspecific, but in the common imagination: what popular Mystery play would be without an apple tree? An apple also caused the Trojan war when young Paris was given the impossible task of rewarding the most beautiful goddess with an apple. Old Norse tales pitch the fruit as the food that keeps the gods young. Isn't our own motto an echo of this — an apple a day keeps the doctor away. And it's not just the fruit, but the trees. Hushed with lichen and the gentle silence of growth, orchards have always been very special places. The word orchard, means fruit garden.

Old orchards are listeners in a world of talkers.

We knelt down on the wooden bridge and peered into the reeds. Something was in there, but what exactly? At first the consensus was that some coots were foraging through the vegetation; then we heard a *chewing* sound and watched as one after the other, reeds were pulled into the watery undergrowth and munched. A scurry, a splash, and at last the water vole revealed itself. The round ball of deep brown fur stood on the bank for a moment then, streamlining itself into a long, thin fur boat, swam beneath us. Its eyes shone like blackberries as it doggy-paddled by. When Kenneth Grahame penned *The Wind in the Willows,* he would have been heartbroken to know that a century after publishing, numbers of this wonderful rodent, the inspiration for his immortal boatman Ratty, would have plummeted by ninety-five per cent. But he would also have found great hope in the London Wetland Centre where we encountered our water vole. Here, right in the middle of the ecological dead zone of one of the world's largest cities, *The Wind in the Willows* pastoral has been recreated. Once this site merely held four concrete reservoirs, now its pools and winding water-corridors are home to thousands of these voles, not to mention the geese, ducks and dragonflies. The water, inlet from the nearby Thames, is as clear as a mountain spring.

Every ditch, every drain, every sewer dreams of being a scene in The Wind in the Willows.

Woken before dawn by an unearthly screeching, I stumbled to the window. Had an owl caught a hare? Or worse? The shrieking grew louder. It sounded like a *human* massacre. 'Pigs,' my nephew informed me the next day. 'They've just moved into Robson's farm. Weaners.' The squealing weaners, youngsters recently separated from the sows, were missing their mothers. Since then they've gradually settled. Of all animals the pig's voice is closest to ours. Our natures aren't entirely dissimilar either. A roving eye that misses little, a gusto for the trough and a cherished dedication for wallowing. No wonder George Orwell, in his animal and human classic *Animal Farm,* made pigs and humans interchangeable in the roles of both visionary and totalitarian despot. My favourite pigs in our locale can be found on Thornhill. To get there you must step out of the twenty-first century. The narrow, grass-grown, traffic-less road gently winds up a hill and then ambles through a small farm. The pigs will be the first things you encounter. These black and white saddlebacks have the run of the place. Forever sniffing and rooting around in every corner, they're all floppy ears, snout and gathering bulk. When I passed through the farm the other day, one pig greeted me like a dog. Wonderfully peaceable animals when allowed to be who they are, pigs have a gift for coexistence and motherhood. If Orwell had met the Thornhill saddlebacks, I wonder whether he would he have changed the characterisation of his pigs?

*

Where would you like to take your favourite author or historical figure?

We all know how the film footage runs. The sound of honking draws the camera to a sky bruised with autumn, and then we see the geese. The flock stays in shot for a while, their beautiful, seemingly effortless skein rippling over the world. Returning to the ground, the camera finds the human face looking upwards, wistful with the unspoken thought — another year has somehow slipped by. We were on the front drive when we heard the geese. There they were, hundreds of feet up. Their faint cries formed a gentle music of two-note calls. Less a honking than the sound of the seasons changing. Were they Pink-footed Geese on their way down to the waterlands of Norfolk? If so they must think they've reached the Promised Land; the temperature in Spitzbergen, an island to the north of Norway where many of our Pink-footed Geese come from, is currently minus six degrees. Having survived the hungry wiles of arctic foxes, polar bears and arctic gales whipping down from frozen mountains, they find themselves in a land of soft ground and autumn trees still in leaf. How do they make their way here so faithfully? By the sun perhaps. Or a collective memory, a recollection of which sea currents and rivers to steer by. A folklore of seascapes and landmarks that they share as they fly. A tale of water, mountains and even pylons.

Who knows what marvels you can witness, just by standing at your front door?

The rain was soft and gentle, the ground pleasantly yielding, and every few yards we came across stunning fungi. The ink cap mushrooms growing right in the middle of the path did indeed seem to contain ink, which, judging by the spills, might have just been used by some woodland writer in a fit of literary inspiration. A little further on we passed through some birches whose trunks were studded with what looked like steps. These are birch bracket fungi. Apparently edible, though very strong of flavour, they were found in the pouch of Ötzi the iceman, a naturally-preserved mummy of a man from about 3400BC. Whether he carried the fungus as an antibiotic food or to sharpen his tools, is not clear. Birch bracket fungi are also known as razor strop because barbers used them to keep their blades keen. Our path through the autumn afternoon took us between high banks bristling with spectacular plates of red toadstool. Fly agaric fungi are poisonous, although through the years, the poor of Europe have devised ways of rendering them edible through careful boiling, thus making famine food. Impressive fungi of enamel red and white spots, I wouldn't be surprised if the genius who first coined the term 'toadstool' was inspired by seeing a fly agaric. On we went, wondering what the next mushroom would be; revelling in one of autumn's many consolations.

Closer to the animal than the plant kingdom, fungi are another one of the world's ordinary enigmas.

We visit him every Saturday morning after our weekly swim. My five-year-old son and I come out of the swimming baths, cross the carpark and run down the grassy bank to the beck. The beck is narrower and shallower than the 'learner' pool we've just been in; yet somewhere in its reeds and weeds and rippling flows, there lurks a monster. A pike. When we first glimpsed this huge fish here, we thought it was a branch snagged on the reeds. Then suddenly it had moved *against* the current. Rising to the surface it grew an elegant bottle nose, a deft flex of fluttering fins and a green, gold and blue body. This solitary lurker of an animal is much maligned. Pike are supposed to be rapacious and savage. True, they hunt efficiently, spurting out from hiding places to catch their prey, but their actions keep the waterways clean: they also eat dead and dying fish, which otherwise would contaminate the water. Much of the time, a pike waits dreaming, as Ted Hughes wrote, of being a dragonfly. Is it their size that contributes to their mythic status? A pond drained in London is reputed to have yielded a fish almost five-foot long. Or is it the mystery of their origin? Monks were long credited with the introduction of pike to Britain, but ancient remains found recently on the Yorkshire coast suggest they swam here thousands of years ago when we were connected to Europe, and the Thames was a tributary of the Rhine.

Thirteen years on, I checked the beck. A pike lurked in exactly the same place. The original fish?

The huge white bird sailed overhead. Long neck coiled into an S shape, wide wings flaring, long legs trailing, it passed across the valley like a spotlight. I wasn't the only onlooker lost in wonder. A mild-mannered Hereford bull, grazing with his cows, looked up and watched the strange sight too. Colossal, brilliant white and languid in flight, it had to be a Great White Egret. Great White Egret! Could it really be this rare vagrant? Over the past decades other members of the egret family have been moving north into Britain from Europe, Little Egrets are now commonplace, and even Cattle Egrets with their golden top knots are becoming less rare, but only a handful of Great White Egrets are spotted each autumn. I waited in case the bird came back, but only sooty black Rooks scattered themselves over the sky. Without this magnificent, floodlit white heron, the late October afternoon seemed already to have darkened into evening. Getting on my bike I raced home. Was there someone else to confirm the sighting? A quick search on the internet gave me my answer. Yesterday, a Great White Egret had been spotted at the nearby Yearsley fish ponds. As though dazzled by the bird, all night I could still see its shimmering gleam as it travelled over the fields from the lake, transfiguring the little valley.

*

It was like seeing an angel.

One by one the colours of autumn have faded. Only the orange of the larches remains, curled round the nose of the hill like a fox's tail. And the bright flames of the beech trees, whose leaves stay longest on the branch. Cycling up the hill I could see the beech avenue. Each tree was like a roaring fire. I always look forward to this part of the journey where the road threads this woody tunnel. A lovely, lonely stretch of tarmac, but today I was not alone. As I coasted through the living colonnade, a mass of small birds looked up at me from the ground beneath these gentle giants. Looked up but didn't scatter. They were too busy eating to take fear from the bike. Even though I stopped, the meal went on uninterrupted. Nuthatches, often secretive, were tucking into the beech mast only yards away. I could see the power of their beaks, and the striking texture of their smoky-blue back. In amongst them were the black-capped Marsh Tits. Even experts can only separate Marsh Tits from their practically identical relative, the Willow Tit, by what they eat. Willow Tits don't care for beech mast. A scutter in the leaf litter revealed a handful of mice, mouths pouched with fodder. With human help, beech trees can live for a millennium.

The wedding party of life is full of fascinating guests — why not go and mingle?

I took another step and from the thick, tussocky grass at my feet a ball of the most beautiful chestnut hues rose and flew silently to the woods. The Woodcock is perhaps the most beautiful of all wading birds. Its eyes are a pair of sloe berries, its plumage a study of mottled browns and cream that are the perfect woodland camouflage. They are usually only seen in the spring when they fly over their territories in a ritual known as *roding,* a twilight beating of the bounds in which rounded wings and long thin beak form a breath-taking silhouette as though the spirit of the woods has briefly taken shape. At other times they are highly secretive. It has only recently become generally known that these forest-dwelling birds, like some arboreal version of the penguin, usually carries its young tucked between its legs and body, piloting them safely through thick and thorny undergrowth. During the *roding,* Woodcocks fly slowly and call loudly in a kind of hoarse bark but today the flight was silent and quick as the falling dusk. Once I found a dead Woodcock. It had been shot through the heart. The beak, as sensitive a piece of equipment as anything technology could ever devise, was gaping slightly. To be able to shoot something so beautiful, I thought, a gunman must really hate himself.

Why are we so quick to destroy the nature that does so much to heal us?

For everything, a season. Tree planting time is here again. As I set off over the bridleway, the wind cut through me. Rain squalls rasped my face. Fallen leaves raced each other. Strange to be thinking of new life just when everything seems to be dying. As I dug the holes, my trowel rang like a bell as it struck different objects. Mostly it was just ordinary stones. *Ordinary*? How long had they lain in the silence here? Ten years, twenty, two hundred, two million? I also excavated some fossils — relics of the Jurassic seas that once covered this land. And then there was the red brick rubble I disinterred. Had there been a building here in the middle of nowhere? Even something as simple as digging a hole for a tree embroils you in mystery. At the woods I cut half a dozen willow whips. Planting them was easy enough, you just poked the wands into the prepared site. Each a yard long, eventually they'll be taller than a house. If lucky, they might see the twenty-fourth century. Goat willows are excellent at growing from such cuttings, providing you water them well for a couple of years. When their low-leaning branches touch the ground, they take root and become separate trees. If left to themselves, the goat willows would have 'walked' here in a century or so anyway. I was just speeding up the process.

The best time to plant a tree is twenty years ago, the second best time is now.

It's hard to stay untouched by the sadness of November. Bare trees, rotting leaves, low skies and shortening days. The hills were white with snow and a thin wind harried me as I walked into town. A death in the family deepened the gloom. Although it was only three o'clock, night was gathering. I was passing under an avenue of dripping lime trees when I heard the palaver. High up in the trees, a flock of Starlings was gathering. Whistling, chirtling, chortling, cheeping, beaks open, heads thrown back they babbled in the dimming late afternoon. They weren't doing anything in particular; this wasn't one of their stunning murmurations, nor were they dressed in their famous iridescent summer breeding plumage, they were just being their chatty, sociable, shaggy selves as they got ready to roost. Stopping, I stared up. More of them arrived filling the empty branches. The resident UK population of Starlings is boosted at this time of year by migrants and I didn't know where this commune had come from, whether they were born and raised in the roofs and back gardens of our small town or whether they'd just arrived from Scandinavia, or perhaps Lithuania. It didn't matter. They were here and they were pulsing with life, the perfect public decorations for a dank November street. With companions like these, I knew that the dark times can't last forever.

In the midst of death we are in life.

Acknowledgements

Thanks to *The Tablet* magazine for the wonderful years of writing this column. In particular, thanks to editors Catherine Pepinster and Brendan Walsh. Thanks to Daniel O'Leary. And to my agent Robert Kirby. Big thanks to the Royal Literary Fund.

About the author

Jonathan Tulloch lives in North Yorkshire with his wife and son. He is a nature writer and novelist. He has written eight novels, including his first, *The Season Ticket*, and his most recent, *Larkinland*. He has won the Betty Trask and J.P Priestley Prizes. His work has been filmed, staged, translated, and serialised on Radio 4. He writes the 'Glimpses of Eden' column in *The Tablet*, and the 'Nature Notebook' in *The Times*. Jonathan plays in the ceilidh band, Herd on the Hill, with his wife, son and uncle. He runs a weekly literature group with asylum seekers in Middlesbrough.